PSYCHOLOGY OF EMOTIONS, MOTIVATIONS AND ACTIONS

HUMOR, STRESS, AND HEALTH

PSYCHOLOGY OF EMOTIONS, MOTIVATIONS AND ACTIONS

Additional books in this series can be found on Nova's website under the Series tab.

Additional E-books in this series can be found on Nova's website under the E-books tab.

PSYCHOLOGY RESEARCH PROGESS

Additional books in this series can be found on Nova's website under the Series tab.

Additional E-books in this series can be found on Nova's website under the E-books tab.

PSYCHOLOGY OF EMOTIONS, MOTIVATIONS AND ACTIONS

HUMOR, STRESS, AND HEALTH

DAVE KOROTKOV
MIHAILO PERUNOVIC
MARVIN CLAYBOURN
AND
IAN FRASER

Nova Science Publishers, Inc.

New York

LIBRARY OF CONGRESS CATALOGING-IN-PUBLICATION DATA

Humor, stress and health / Dave Korotkov ... [et al.].
   p. cm.
 Includes bibliographical references and index.
 ISBN 978-1-61209-776-3 (softcover)
 1. Laughter. 2. Wit and humor--Health aspects. 3. Stress (Psychology) 4.
Health. I. Korotkov, Dave.
 BF575.L3H86 2011
 152.4'3--dc22
                            2011002553

Published by Nova Science Publishers, Inc. ✝ *New York*

DEDICATIONS

In memory of my honor's supervisor, Dr. John Lavery of Brock University (St. Catharines, Ontario, Canada) who supported me during my first research project linking humor to health.
To my brother Peter for your good cheer during a year that is best forgotten.
To Sven Svebak, Rod Martin, and Herbert Lefcourt for having the wisdom to see the value of humor in day-to-day life and for developing a research program that in the end, addresses our assumptions surrounding mirth.

Dave Korotkov

For my family
Mihalio Perunovic

For Chad, whose patience in the face of my embarrassingly long work days I appreciate more than words can express. I promise it won't continue forever.

Marvin Claybourn

To those who continually make me laugh and for those who approach each day with a light heart.

Ian Fraser

CONTENTS

PREFACE

Much of contemporary psychological research on humor is based on the assumption that a sense of humor is a positive and desirable personality characteristic that enhances psychological health and well-being. Researchers generally assume that individuals with a greater sense of humor possess a number of other desirable traits, such as great optimism, self-acceptance, self-confidence, and autonomy. Humorous people are also thought to be able to cope more effectively with stress, to generally experience less negative moods such as depression and anxiety, to enjoy greater physical health, and to have more positive and healthy relatinships with others (Kuiper & Olinger, in press). In recent years, these positive views of humor have given rise to a burgeoning "humor and health" movement whose proponents, through workshops, seminars, and popular books, seek to promote greater expression of humor in schools, hospitals, psychotherapy settings, and the workplace. These ideas have also gained wide attention in the popular media, where magazine articles and television programs frequently extol the benefits of humor and laughter (p. 159)......Although proponents of the "humor and health" movement would agree with the idea that some forms of humor are unhealthy (focusing particularly on jokes that are not "politically correct"), little rigorous theoretical or empirical work has been done to provide guidelines for identifying exactly when humor is healthy and when it is unhealthy. This is an area that needs further work. In the meantime, overly enthusisastic and uncritical endorsements of humor of whatever sort as contributing to psychological well-being are unwarranted (p. 178).

-Kuiper and Martin (1998)

Is laughter good medicine? Is humor socially beneficial? Can we teach people to be more humorous and to laugh in a wide range of situations? What do we actually mean when we say that a person has a good sense of humor? Should laughter, smiling, and perhaps amusement be included in our definition? Should we use the "Fun Philosophy" in our work setting to coincide with our labor or should humor, fun, and work be kept separate? Whether the benefits of humor are as popular culture depicts them, these and many other questions have captured philosophers, researchers, theorists, and the general public's attention over the centuries. For researchers, the early work of *Sigmund Freud, Norman Cousins'* physical plight in the 1970s, and subsequently, of scholars *Sven Svebak, Rod Martin*, and *Herbert Lefcourt* in the early 1970s and 1980s, respectively, and of *Willibald Ruch* in the early 1990s, seems to have set the stage and influenced the research agendas for numerous scholars and budding or self-proclaimed comedians within the academy and beyond. To be certain, as the opening quotes point out, one should not forget the well intentioned though often misguided role of the media and self-help authors in extolling the virtues of humor. As Kuiper and Martin wisely suggest above, we need to be wary until the evidence suggests otherwise.

Our own interests in researching, understanding, using, and applying humor are quite varied, with each of us bringing a different perspective to the table, so to speak. In reflecting on my own (DK) interests surrounding the sense of humor construct, I have always been struck (okay, not literally) and impressed (and somewhat envious) at an individual's ability to make others laugh. Whether we discuss humor appreciation or liking, motivation, laughter, joke construction, imitation/parody, or when we watch our favorite sitcom or comedy, humor has a way of distracting us from the day-to-day unpleasantries - or so it seems. Humor may also reinforce our behaviors. To be sure, humor can also bring us together or it can tear us apart. Thus, in the wise words of my friend Les Myers (Brock University, St. Catharines, Ontario) from days gone by, a good philosophy is to "take life seriously *but* not solemnly." But I digress somewhat. Others were also significant in those comedian-wannabe, formative years of mine such as family, friends, and even strangers. Little did I think back then that these individuals would be instrumental in laying the groundwork for my own admittedly, quirky, and self-critical sense of humor, and not to forget, research agenda. In any case, I was so struck by the relevance of humor in day-to-day social interaction that I started my own humor research agenda as an undergraduate (e.g., Korotkov, 1991), shortly after Rod Martin and Herbert Lefcourt (1984) published a series of impressive studies linking humor to stress and mood. I later followed this up by looking at the role of coping humor in relation to stress and physical symptomatology (Korotkov & Hannah, 1994).

For Mihailo and Marvin, the importance of humor can be found in its applications to the social relations realm, and the clinical context, respectively. For Mihailo, humor is is an everyday *tool* that is used to help initiate, develop, and mend relationships or as Mihailo might put it jokingly, "to put up fences." It also doesn't hurt that Mihailo brings a wealth of knowledge on the psychology of relationships to this team. As a clinician, Marvin sees the benefits of humor by encouraging his patients to build more fun into their lives in order to help manage stress, anxiety, and depression. Personally, his self-deprecating humor style has immense value in helping him and others to minimize stress. For both him and his clients, it is preventative in minimizing the complexity of an already tiring lifestyle. For Ian, apart from his judicious use of humor and fun-seeking in his own life, he brings us a wealth of knowledge on the role of humor in the teaching process (e.g., Fraser & Fraser, 2010). As Ian's research indicates and as many comedians can attest to, you need to know your audience. One also needs to know how beneficial humor can be and in what contexts. In the latter case, more research is certainly needed. Our text is geared somewhat in this direction.

More to the point, one of our interests concerns the measurement and experience of humor and laughter to help us understand its impact on stress, ill-health, and well-being. To this end, we describe three studies herein linking a short version of Martin and Lefcourt's (1984) Situational Humor Response Questionnaire (SHRQ) to a host of psychosocial variables. In achieving this goal, we first provide a review of the humor literature, in particular the role of arousal, incongruity, superiority, and behavioral theories or models in helping us understand this unique human attribute and experience. We then describe the SHRQ and of course, our rationale. Three studies are then reported to help validate the brief scale. In these studies, separate samples of participants were administered the SHRQ, several other humor and laughter measures, as well as scales related to daily stress, mood, personality, coping, and perceived physical symptomatology or illness behavior. The results from these studies indicated that, with few notable exceptions, the 12-item version was comparable in performance to the 21-item version; it also appeared to be capable of detecting stress moderating effects and in other cases, direct effects on well-being. Moreover, we found the SHRQ to be correlated with higher levels of extraversion, agreeableness, various coping styles (e.g., positive reframing), self-enhancing and affiliative humor styles, life satisfaction, optimism, happiness, vigor, positive mood, negative mood, and stress. The correlates of humor and laughter are indeed fascinating.

This brief document may be of some use to those interested in learning more about the humor phenomenon and to validate what they already know. In this respect, one additional and novel aspect of this text (okay, we're not so modest) is the inclusion of the behavioral model of humor in the theories and models section. Relatively little has been written about the behavioral aspects of humor and what research there is, appears to be scattered. Whether this is due to a zeitgeist in which humor tends to be considered a trait, the relatively objective nature of behaviorism (depending on whether we include social-cognitive theories in this discussion), or the difficulty in studying, measuring, and replicating behavior or humor idiographically, the latter (i.e., behaviorism) may turn, perhaps, an otherwise interesting topic into a potentially dull read – but we suspect not. In any case, behaviorism or applied behavior analysis has expanded in recent years, in particular with the development of positive behavioral support. With this addition, we can now broaden the pool of hypotheses to help reflect on the varied functions of humor, in tandem with the other theories. To be sure, the theories are somewhat isomorphic to one another.

And finally, the text may be of benefit to graduate students, faculty, undergraduates, as well as professionals in the fields of social work, nursing/medicine, and business, to name but a handful of disciplines. To this end, we hope that you will find this material interesting and somewhat fascinating, much as we did in putting this document together. We look forward to any comments you may have regarding this text.

Chapter 1

INTRODUCTION

"Laughter is the best medicine, says the old adage − but how much truth is there to the saying?"

                    - Mindess, Miller, Turek, Bender, & Corbin (1985, p. 109)

Since comedy is − again − in some way about tragedy, one of its functions is to alleviate the pain we would constantly be suffering were we to concentrate on the tragedy that characterizes life on this planet. Humor is a social lubricant that helps us get over some of the bad spots. It is a humanizing agent. You know, it's strange − we will accept almost any allegation of our deficiencies − cosmetic, intellectual, virtuous − save one, the charge that we have no sense of humor.

                    - Allen (in Allen & Wollman, 1998, p. viii)

The current vogue surrounding the therapeutic consequences of humor and laughter owes much to the ascent of holistic medicine in the 1970s, as well as to Norman Cousins' incredible story about his recovery from a disabling disease. In 1976, Cousins chronicled his trials with the potentially fatal disorder, Ankylosing Spondylitis, a chronic, inflammatory, collagen disease of the connective tissue. His story was subsequently published in the 1979 book, *Anatomy of an Illness as Perceived by the Patient: Reflections on Healing and Regeneration* (see also Goldstein,

1987, p. 2). While hospitalized and in considerable pain, Cousins found hospital routines to be additional stressors that appeared to exacerbate his condition. Realizing that such a negative atmosphere could only worsen his state, and with the aid and cooperation of his physician, Cousins moved out of the hospital and sought his own antidote: humor and vitamin C. Therapy consisted of watching old movie clips of Candid Camera, the Marx Brothers, and reading humorous books, while ingesting massive doses of vitamin C. The apparent effect of this treatment was astounding. According to Cousins (1979),

> It worked. I made the joyous discovery that 10 minutes of belly laughter had an anesthetic effect and would give me at least two-hours of pain-free sleep. When the pain-killing effect of the laughter wore off, we would switch on the motion-picture projector again, and, not infrequently it would lead to another pain-free sleep interval.

While Cousins' cause-effect claims concerning the apparent health enhancing effects of humor and laughter could easily be dismissed given other alternative explanations (e.g., history, regression to the mean; see Cook & Campbell, 1979), the holistic value of humor and laughter was just beginning to be considered a serious subject of research for many scholars (e.g., Cann, Holt, & Calhoun, 1999; Kuiper & Nicholl, 2004; Lefcourt & Martin, 1986; Martin, 2001; Martin & Lefcourt, 1983; Saraglou & Scariot, 2002; Simon, 1988; Svebak, 1974; Svebak, Jensen, & Götestam, 2008; Tümkaya, 2007). For example, there is now a journal devoted exclusively to the study of humor (Humor: International Journal of Humor Research), scholarly societies and associations (e.g., The International Society for Humor Studies), humor and humor writing improvement courses/programs and books (Allen & Wollman, 1998; Klein, 1989; Nevo, Aharonson, & Klingman, 1998; Peter & Dana, 1982; Rakel & Hedgecock, 2008), as well as a keen multidisciplinary interest from scholars in such areas as psychology (e.g., Comisky, Crane, & Zillmann, 1980; Ziv, 1979), anthropology (e.g., Apte, 1985; Butovskaya & Kozintsev, 1996), linguistics (e.g., Oring, 1992; Salvatore, 1994), computer science (e.g.,

Dormann & Biddle, 2006; Mihalcea & Strapparava, 2006), communication studies (e.g., Brock, 2004; Meyer, 1997), biology (e.g., Fry, 1994; Watson, Matthews, & Allman, 2007), sociology (e.g., Zijderveld, 1995; Kulpers, 2006), social work (e.g., Mik-Mayer, 2007; Moran & Hughes, 2006), politics (e.g., Lewis, 2006; Morris, 2009), business (Lee & Lim, 2008; Rogerson-Revell, 2007), and nursing (e.g., Dean, 1997; Hulse, 1994; Simon, 1988). As Martin et al. (2003) point out, the study of humor is also likely to garner increased attention in light of several recent developments in the growing area of positive psychology (e.g., Peterson & Seligman, 2004; see also Martin, 2003).

Although the history of humor and health research is replete with other landmark moments (e.g., Freud, 1905; Svebak, 2010; see Martin, 2007, p. 20 for a fascinating history of humor), a second key and relatively recent event occurred only a few years post-Cousins with the publication of a series of studies by Martin and Lefcourt (1983, 1984; see also Lefcourt & Martin, 1986) on the sense of humor as a stress and mood modifier. In their research, Martin and Lefcourt found that humor and laughter were linked to the attenuation of the relationship between life stress and mood disturbance. Since their classic set of studies, other researchers have come forth to proclaim both the virtues and vices of mirth (see e.g., Abel, 1998, 2002; Beermann & Ruch, 2009; Friedman et al., 1995; Friedman et al., 1993; Guiliani, McRae, & Gross, 2008; Kerkkänen, Kuiper, & Martin, 2004; Martin et al., 2002; Moran & Hughes, 2006; Svebak, 2010; Svebak, Kristofferson, & Aasarød, 2006).

Despite some claims or qualifications to the contrary which we discuss throughout this text (e.g., Boyle & Joss-Reid, 2004; Kuiper & Nicholl, 2004; Martin, 2001, 2002), the view that humor and laughter produce therapeutic effects on health by reducing stress has been well received (e.g., Burridge, 1978; Cassell, 1973; Ellis, 1977; Martin, 2002; McGhee, 1979, p. 227; Nehemour, McClusky-Fawcell, & McGhee, 1986). For example, Cassell (1974) had suggested that humor could be used as a monitoring tool for evaluating the efficacy of therapy, client progress, and a client's reaction to the environment. Cassell further suggests that humor could serve as an aid in the coping process. Albert Ellis (1977), the founder of rational-emotive-behavior therapy, suggests that humor can help to minimize cognitive, behavioral, and emotional distress. Cognitively, humor lends insight to the inflexible or rigid client. Behaviorally, it encourages relaxation and reduces anxiety. Emotively, it brings enjoyment and pleasure, and helps the client to construe life more positively. From a psychodynamic perspective, Zwerling (1955; cited in Haig, 1988, p. 142) has suggested that the therapeutic use of the *Favorite Joke Technique* helps to understand the patients' inner conflicts. Aaron Beck (1981; cited in Haig, 1988, pp. 147-148) has suggested that a therapists' exaggerated demonstration of a patients' faulty thinking may encourage the person to "loosen the belief system and promote cognitive dissonance, which might result in the patient seeking alternative ideas." Further, humor has the potential to distract the patient from painful affect. It is also believed that humor and laughter may be of some benefit in family and marital therapy. For example, according to Zuk (1964; cited in Haig, 1988, p. 151), laughter serves the following functions in family therapy:

1) Reaffirms allegiances between family members.
2) Discounts or qualifies a dialogue.
3) Defends against intrusions by individuals outside the family system.
4) Expresses pleasure.
5) Signals that there is a secret to be kept from the therapist.
6) Expresses helplessness and discourages demands by others.
7) Signals or covers anxiety in the individual or family, particularly in the absence of humor.

Along similar lines, in a literature review by Martin (2002; see also Martin, 2001 and Svebak, Martin, & Holmen, 2004), humor and laughter may extend their effects on physical health through four possible mechanisms: (1) through systemic physiological change (e.g., production of endorphins); (2) through positive affective states (e.g., positive mood, joy); (3) through stress moderation; and (4) by raising social support levels to help buffer stress.[1] The following theories, though not fully inclusive, elaborate on some of these processes and effects.

THEORIES OF HUMOR: AROUSAL, INCONGRUITY, SUPERIORITY/DISPARAGEMENT, AND BEHAVIORAL

> On a golf course, one golfer is choking another to death. A third golfer nonchalantly walks over and says to the aggressor, "Pardon me, sir, but your grips all wrong."
>
> - Gollob & Levine (1967)

In their book, *Humor and Life Stress: Antidote to Adversity*, Lefcourt and Martin (1986; see also Berger, 2010, Ferguson & Ford, 2008, Haig, 1988, and Martin, 2007, pp. 31-82) categorized several theories of humor according to Eysenck's (1942) 3-type classification model of affect, cognition, and conation (motivation).[2] Within each system (i.e., arousal, incongruity, superiority/disparagement and behavioral), varying degrees of emphasis are placed on these components. Although these theories address different aspects of humor and laughter, the classificatory types (i.e., theories) nonetheless do not reflect the total humor experience. For example, the behavioral implications, consequences, and antecedents (e.g., stimulus control and behavioral function) of humor and laughter as well as various phenomenological processes (e.g., cognitive appraisal; see e.g., Dixon, 1980 and Vollrath, 2001) are only alluded to, rather than objectively spelled out, across these models. Nor are the functional aspects of behavior clearly articulated. Thus, to complement our discussion, and given its prominence as a model for understanding individual behavior idiographically, we also include the behavioral model as a fourth potential explanatory framework. In particular, inclusion of the behavioral model in

---

[1] According to Martin (2002), these mechanisms have yet to be adequately tested. Further theoretical and methodologically rigorous studies need to be conducted.

[2] We define humor and laughter in the section that follows.

this discussion allows an additional means for conceptualizing the creation, experience, and maintenance or stability of the humor and laughter responses, as well as the functional reasons and generalization (and maintenance) of such responses.

(i) Arousal Theories

The first category reflects the view of those arousal theorists who have argued that humor and laughter reduces physiological arousal or tension in stressful situations; that is, humor and laughter can modify one's perception or construal and felt experience of arousal (e.g., Freud, 1905, 1928).[3] One significant theoretical model comes from the comprehensive work of Sigmund Freud (1905, 1928; see also Apter & Smith, 1977, Berlyne, 1972, Dixon, 1980, Kline, 1977, Lazarus & Folkman, 1984, Vaillant, 2000, and Wyer & Collins, 1992 for other arousal based models). In general, Freud presented his theory of humor in two distinct publications. The first publication, a book entitled, *Jokes and Their Relation to the Unconscious* (Jokes), was written in 1905 and dealt primarily with four mirth related entities: the joke, wit, the comic, and humor. The second publication was a paper simply entitled, *Humour* (Freud, 1928).[4]

As part of Freud's grander theory of personality, he believed that the structure of personality is configured by three interrelated states or constructs, the id, the ego, and the superego. From this model, Freud (1936) argued that several conflicts can take place between these three structures, one of which involves the id and ego. Technically, the id

---

[3] Consider the inverted-U model where optimal arousal is reflected at mid-point in the curve. Extremes at both ends reflect decrements in the criterion (e.g., pleasure; see Berlyne, 1972); thus the goal is to find the optimal level to enhance one's positive emotional experience.

[4] According to Levine (1969, p. 3), Freud seems to be the only theorist to have viewed humor as a fundamental psychological process that exemplifies one of the two motivational bases for all behavior. Thus, according to Freud, "The dream serves preponderantly to guard against pain while wit serves to acquire pleasure; in these two aims, all of our psychic activities meet" (as cited in Levine, 1969).

(functioning in accordance with the pleasure principle) may give rise to a psychic impulse that needs to be gratified but is barred from expression by the ego (functioning in line with the reality principle). To *filter* the id's demands, the ego employs various defence mechanisms.[5] Humor/laughter reflects one such mechanism(s). That is, we can often more easily handle distress or anxiety if we adopt a humorous or playful attitude (McGhee, 1979, p. 32).

Freud further contended that laughter and comedy are a function of three separate theories based on psychic economy. Generally, Freud believed that comedy helps to release any nervous energy that is built up in the nervous system, with the resultant laughter acting as a release valve (see e.g., Haig, 1988, p. 21). In particular, he was careful to distinguish the wit from the comic, and humor (Grieg, 1969). In considering wit, Freud made reference to various *joke-work* techniques, the intrapsychic phenomena of creating the joke (e.g., condensation; "alcohol-idays"), each of which allows the individual to express forbidden and repressed sexual and aggressive impulses.[6,7] In other words, psychic energy is not expended for inhibition (i.e., it is economized) and pleasure is derived from the gratification of the instinct (see Kline, 1977, p. 9). This description of wit can be seen in the following jokes (see Mindess, Miller, Turek, Bender, & Corbin, 1985): (1) "Is sex dirty? Yes….if its done right" (sex joke); and (2) "Male: What do I have to do to get a kiss? Female: Chloraform" (hostile joke). According to a Freudian analysis, each joke type represents a psychological mechanism or gateway to help satisfy the needs of the id.

The second distinction Freud made was that of the comic. Generally, the comic has to do with the various nonverbal sources of mirth (e.g.,

---

[5] See Vaillant's (2000) discussion of humor as an adaptive and mature defence mechanism

[6] For his 1905 text, Freud borrowed from his widely acclaimed work, *The Interpretation of Dreams* (Sulloway, 1979, p. 356). While reading the proof for *Dreams*, Wilhelm Fliess commented to Freud that his dream analyses were full of jokes. After deliberating on this insight, Freud subsequently proposed that the technical components of jokes were similar to those found in dreams. Thus the analogy between *dream-work* and *joke-work* was born.

[7] As alluded to, joke-work is similar to dream-work, albeit with a number of qualifications. One major difference is that in a joke the meaning must be intelligible, whereas in a dream the meaning is meant to be hidden.

slapstick comedy) in which the observer of the actor experiences a build up of psychic energy, while expecting the expected to occur (e.g., "To be a good nurse, you must be absolutely sterile"; Klein, 1989). Laughter ensues when the unexpected occurs or when the expected does not happen. With the comic, it is the mental or ideational energy that is saved as opposed to inhibitory energy as in wit or the joke. In sum, the pleasure of the comic lies in the economy of expenditure in thought (Grieg, 1969, p. 273).

The final and most relevant distinction that Freud made, was that of humor. While wit represents a savings of inhibitory energy, the comic, mental or ideational energy, humor represents an economizing of emotional or affective energy. Essentially, when confronted with adversity the ability to perceive humorous elements in the situation or to view the situation from an altered perspective, allows one to discharge psychic energy in the form of laughter. Humor therefore diverts the distressful affect from conscious attention.[8] Put differently, when confronted with an intense situation, some of this primed emotion is suddenly diverted, thus freeing the psychic energy as laughter. Humor tries to withdraw the idea of painful affect from one's conscious or mindful attention. When this happens, it overcomes the defence automatism (see Grieg, 1969). In this sense, humor is a defence mechanism that allows one to see the funny side of a stressful encounter (e.g., accident). An example of this gallows type of humor (see also *Broken Humor*; Haig, 1988, p. 22) is exemplified in the case of a murderer who is about to be hanged. When asked if he has any

---

[8] Interestingly, when Freud was asked to sign a sworn statement as a requirement to leave Nazi Germany, he slyly invoked the power of humor through his *play on words*. Richard Simon Keller (1977) graphically illustrates this in the following:

"I, Prof. Freud, hereby confirm that after the Anschluss of Austria to the German Reich, I have been treated by the German authorities and particularly by the Gestapo, with all the respect and consideration due to my scientific reputation, that I could live and work in full freedom, that I could continue to pursue my activities in every way I desired, that I found full support from all concerned in this respect, and that I have not the slightest reason for any complaint." Earnest Jones, who reports this incident in his biography of Freud, and was himself instrumental in getting Freud out of Austria, explains "Freud had, of course, no compunction about signing it, but he asked if he might be allowed to add a sentence which was: "I can heartily recommend the Gestapo to anyone."

last words, the murderer replies, "Could I have a scarf for my neck, I don't want to catch cold?"

In sum, Freud's theories of wit, the comic, and humor represent three distinct explanations or psychic mechanisms of mirthfulness with each emphasizing the notion of economy of expenditure. Respectively, these economies are of inhibition (wit), upon ideation or through cathexis (comic), and finally, of affect (humor). While his theory offers some intriguing hypotheses and appears to be the most impressive single volume devoted to a psychological analysis of humor (Kline, 1977), support for Freud's theory is limited and inconsistent. While some analytic research continues, the psychoanalytic theory of humor has been largely abandoned. However, as Martin (2007, p. 41; see also Martin, 1998) emphasizes, early tests of Freud's theory tended to focus less on humor, a model with significant implications for the stress-coping process. Further, there appears to be some indirect support for various aspects of Freud's model.

Just as Freud's model can be construed as based on arousal (tension) reduction, other arousal based models are of value here. For example, evidence from Berlyne's important work (e.g., 1972) provides additional support for the arousal perspective. Basing his work on the inverted-U model, Berlyne argued that an optimal level of arousal is associated with high levels of pleasure. However, as Martin (2007, p. 62) further points out, while arousal appears to be linearly related to emotional enjoyment, there is little support for the inverted-U relationship between arousal and pleasure. Berlyne's work is important for its support of humor as a "complex, physiological-based interaction between cognition and emotion."

(ii) Incongruity Theories

The second set of theories, those related to the incongruity model, focuses on cognition and less on the socio-emotional aspects of humor. Incongruity theorists have contended that humor is healthy because it allows one to broaden, modify, or shift perspective away from, for example, a demanding or stressful encounter. By shifting perspective, one *distances* the self from the distressing event. Thus, humor is a function of the juxtaposition, reframing, or restructuring of two normally different or disparate ideas, concepts, or situations in an unexpected manner (Lefcourt & Martin, 1986, p. 9). Koestler (1964) echoes this theme through his *Theory of Bisociation*. According to Koestler, bisociation refers to "the juxtaposition of two normally incongruous frames of reference or the discovery of various similarities and analogies implicit in concepts normally considered remote from each other." Consider the following joke, which demonstrates this juxtaposition: "I used to snore so loud that I would wake myself up. But I solved the problem. Now I sleep in the next room" (last sentence or punchline reflects a shift away from or violation of expectation; Mindess et al., 1985).[9]

Similarly, O'Connell (1976; see also Abel, 2002, Kant, 1790, Nerhardt, 1976, and Suls, 1983) has argued that humor is beneficial because it allows the individual to distance him- or herself from a tension provoking situation. By distancing oneself, the individual changes his or her frame of reference (reframing), thereby minimizing one's negative experience of the stressful encounter. Similarly, from a transactional perspective, humor may affect the stress process in two possible ways (see e.g., Lazarus & Folkman, 1984).[10] First, it is believed that those with a strong sense of humor would be more likely to appraise the situation in a less threatening or more benign way (primary appraisal). And second, humor may act as a coping strategy (secondary appraisal) to help minimize

---

[9] Koestler further believed that humor, scientific discovery, and art were each a function of bisociation. The reason why humor elicits laughter while art and scientific discovery do not, has more to do with the emotional context or situation in which these activities normally take place or occur. While art and science are elicited in neutral or positive emotional contexts, humor can be brought on by aggression or low-grade anxiety.

[10] Wiebe and Fortenberry (2006, p. 137) also discuss a third, dynamic approach in relation to personality in general, whereby certain personality traits may give rise to specific life events. The life events, may also influence personality. For example, individuals who self-describe as neurotic are more likely to *prompt* negative events to occur in their lives. Extrapolating, perhaps humorous individuals are more likely to cue certain positive or negative events, depending on for example, one's humor style (e.g., affiliative vs. aggressive; see Martin et al., 2003 for a discussion concerning humor styles).

any negative or distressful affect. This view of humor and its purported distancing function has been articulated by several writers over the years (Abel, 2002; Dixon, 1980; Kuiper, Martin, & Olinger, 1993; Lefcourt & Thomas, 1998; Martin, 2003, p. 282; O'Connell, 1976; Suls, 1972).

The incongruity model appears to be generally supported as an *essential perspective of humor*. Although incongruity has been difficult to define and there has been some controversy as to whether incongruity resolution is a necessary condition for an affective experience, the model has contributed much to our understanding of the cognitive-perceptual underpinnings of humor (Martin, 2007, p. 72).

(iii) Superiority/Disparagement Theories

Superiority or disparagement theories are among the oldest of the humor theories (e.g., Aristotle, Plato). Generally, these theories suggest that humor enhances feelings of self-control, mastery, self-esteem, and confidence, in addition to minimizing the threat that may accompany a stressful event, demand, or situation. According to this view, one's sense of superiority results from the humorous disparagement of others, including oneself. Thus, in one sense, humor can reflect a form of aggression towards another (male/female, ethnic groups, etc.; Martin, 2007, p.43) or towards the self. One major proponent of this view is Jacob Levine (1977; see also Gruner, 1997). From a developmental perspective, Levine (p. 129) believes that humor is a necessary element in both growth and peak mastery processes. During each stage of development, the child learns that humor is a source or antecedent of pleasure that allows him or her to reexperience the mastery of early life. As an adult, these early sources of gratification and mastery have been consolidated and are more difficult to recognize or detect. Whether an individual is distressed or relaxed, humor represents an assertion of mastery or control over the environment. For example, Levine argues that humor is often used to reduce anxiety. Because humor is thought of as a learned drive, it represents an attempt at mastery (or competence attainment) when experiencing anxiety or tension. For example, consider the joke of the man who is facing a firing squad and is asked if he would like a last cigarette. "He replies, no thanks, I am trying to quit" (p. 130). In this example, it is the man's attempt at quitting that represents his need for mastery or superiority despite the looming threat.

In his critique of the superiority model, Martin (2007, p. 53) points out that while aggression can play a role in humor, little evidence exists concerning the pervasive influence of disparagement in *all* forms of mirth (versus Gruner's, 1997 position). That is, not all forms of humor are based on disparagement. However, while the superiority view has to a large extent been replaced by the incongruity model, the former may still serve some theoretical purpose in helping researchers to understand the impact of humor in mastering life's demands (see our later discussion of social-cognitive theory and humor production).

(iv) Behavioral Models[11]

The last model that may help to shed additional light on the humor and laughter experience reflects a *second force* in psychology, the behavioral approach. Interestingly, despite offering several plausible hypotheses and mechanisms for construing mirthful behavior, there has been relatively little discussion or research concerning the behavioral model (e.g., Haig, 1988, p. 143). While in some ways it may be construed of in a conative or superiority sense (e.g., Levine's model), given for example, the concepts of reinforcement and establishing operations, the behavioral model (e.g., operant perspective) views humor and laughter as learned functions of the environment (e.g., three-term contingency; *antecedent* – humorous cue, *behavior* – joke telling, *consequence* – social laughter/reinforcement → behavioral maintenance and generalization → repeated joke telling; see

---

[11] While one might place the behavioral model within the parameters of the superiority approach, we decided against this on two grounds, the first being the objective nature of the behavioral model and second, the lack of clarity with the former approach in defining behavior. In any case, we find it necessary and useful to bring some clarity and application to humor using this model.

e.g., Epstein & Joker, 2007). Despite little acknowledgment as a viable model to explain individual differences in humor and laughter, its benefits have been recognized, at least somewhat within the clinical context (e.g., the use of humor in systematic desensitization; Richman, 1996; Ventis, Higbee, & Murdock, 2001; see also Cassell, 1973 and Ellis, 1977).[12]

In exploring its implications, the production of humor and laughter can in part be explained by such concepts as the setting event (e.g., positive mood, context), stimulus control (e.g., predictable or antecedent cues to be humorous), and reinforcement (see also establishing operations). For example, a joke produced in the presence of others (i.e., controlling stimuli/discriminative stimuli) may lead to reinforcement (e.g., an observer's smile and/or laughter). However, its behavioral production and reinforcement may theoretically, be modified, strengthened, or weakened by an establishing operation (i.e., abolishing, motivating; e.g., deficit or excess of social contact) or be contextually influenced by a setting event (e.g., humor produced only in response to specific others or when experiencing a positive mood; that is, a discriminant and controlling stimulus). Further, given extinction and spontaneous recovery processes, the production of humor may wax and wane and wax (i.e., intermittent or variable behavior) depending on the presence of various situational cues. Thus, generalization or maintenance of the humor response or its creation may occur spontaneously or through training, and intermittent reinforcement (see e.g., Martin & Pear, 2011, p. 191; see Chart 1 for a brief summary of some possible applications to humor based on the behavioral model).

---

[12] Grossman (1977) makes reference to the reinforcement model, albeit somewhat implicitly. For example, Grossman states,

> It is essential to point out the limitations of the use of jokes. The joke is no more that 'magic pill' than any other therapeutic technique in our armamentarium. The favourite joke is not always directly connected with a patient's problems: on many occasions it may merely be a joke that was heard and repeated with success. The reward of laughter might be enough to make this a joke that the patient might repeat on all occasions. The reward is what makes the joke a favourite and not its personal meaning.

Chart 1. Sample of potential applications of learning concepts to humor and laughter

Concept/Explanation[*]	Example
Stimulus Control: The magnitude of the relationship between a stimulus and a response.	• Telling a joke in the presence of one who is very likely (strong correlation), likely (moderate correlation), somewhat likely (modest correlation), or not likely (uncorrelated) to laugh.
Satiation: A reinforcer that is no longer reinforcing as a result of continuous exposure.	• Excessive laughter in the presence of a comedian leading to, for example, only amusement.
Deprivation: A situation or condition in which an organism has been deprived of or has not experienced a reinforcer. Given a heightened state of deprivation, the reinforcer increases in value.	• When there has been a lack of social contact that would allow for joke telling, the person is more likely to be humorous in the presence of others.
Antecedent/Stimulus: An event or cue that precedes a response or varies in its probability in giving rise to it.	• Watch a sitcom (stimulus or antecedent) to prompt a response (e.g., laughter)
Aversive Stimulus: A stimulus that may decrease (punisher) or increase (negative reinforcer) behavior.	• Being told that one's joke was inappropriate.
Discriminative Stimulus (S^D): A stimulus that signals forthcoming reinforcement from a behavior.	• Telling a joke in the presence of one's spouse or partner; there is a high likelihood of the partner laughing or finding the joke amusing, when we see that person.
S^1*(S-Delta):* A stimulus that signals a response that will not be reinforced.	• A group meeting where others don't share your sense of humor; joke telling ceases when in their presence.
Behavior: Anything that can be seen, heard, and measured.	• Can include any number of humor/laughter related behaviors including joke telling, constructing a joke, smiling, behaviorally expressing amusement, and laughing.
Positive Reinforcer: A stimulus that is presented subsequently to a response with the result of strengthening its response (Frequency, Intensity, Duration)	• A friend who complements you on your sense of humor or smiles/laughs, after you tell a joke. You are more likely to continue with such behavior.
Reprimand: An aversive stimulus presented subsequent to behavior.	• Being told not to tell a sick joke again; try something 'cleaner.'
Behavior Excess: A situation where behavior occurs at a rate greater than normal, appropriate, or desired.	• Excessive laughing or telling the same joke again and again, or engaging in non-stop like joke telling to the exclusion of other social skill behaviors; joke telling behavior beyond the average frequency of others' similar behavior.
Behavior Deficit: A situation where behavior occurs at a rate less than normal, appropriate, or desired.	• Engaging in few humor related behaviors such as joke telling, smiling, or joke perception.

Intermittent Reinforcement: A situation where behavior is reinforced periodically versus continuously.

- Humorous behavior such as imitating or parodying others that is periodically reinforced and which will be difficult to extinguish.

Extinction (operant): The weakening of a previously reinforced behavior through the withholding of a reinforcer.

- When others consistently fail to laugh at a joke after initial reinforcement with a resultant decrease in the telling of that joke.

Spontaneous Recovery: A situation in which a previously extinguished response recurs when exposed to similar stimulus conditions in which the behavior was previously prompted.

- Retelling of an 'old' joke in the presence of another who initially laughed.

Generalization: The extent to which behavior occurs across persons and situations; may occur naturally or as a result of training.

- Telling a joke to similar friends or responding with laughter across a variety of distinct sitcoms.

Stimulus Generalization Gradient: The graphical relationship between varying degrees of stimulus similarity and response. The closer the resemblance to the original stimulus, the greater the likelihood of response.

- Laughing at different comedians whose repertoire is somewhat similar; laughter may decrease given differences in a comedian's repertoire. The same may apply to similar and distinct sitcoms.

Efficacy Expectation/Self-Efficacy: One's belief in their ability to engage in a particular behavior

- Believing that one can tell or construct a joke or make others laugh.

Outcome Expectation: Belief or expectation that a behavior will result in a specific outcome.

- Believing that a particular joke will make others laugh or believing that laughter will lead to positive health outcomes such as mood change and physiological responding.

Vicarious Positive Reinforcement: The reinforcement that results from observers viewed reinforced; this may lead to an increase in behavior.

- Watching a comedy and imitating a particular funny behavior you observed because the comedian was 'apparently' reinforced.

Modeling: Showing or demonstrating a behavior to an individual as a mode of teaching.

- Teaching someone how to parody a popular character or how to construct a joke.

Respondent Behavior: A stimulus (conditioned, unconditioned) that elicits a response.

- Reflexive laughter

Conditioned Stimulus: A stimulus, after being paired with another stimulus, elicits a response.

- A friend who is known to automatically elicit a laughter response; that person was once a neutral stimulus but through conditioning, took on response (e.g., laughter) eliciting or qualities

Conditioned Response: An elicited response brought about by a conditioned stimulus (Pavlovian). It may also be a reinforced response (operant).

- Laughing automatically in response to a humorous friend or comedian; 'seeing' a comedian may cause one to laugh.

Note: *Explanations can be found in a variety of sources including Martin and Pear (2011), Sundel and Sundel (1975, 1993), and Miltenberger (2008).

While these dynamics may reflect the production of humor and laughter and describe its intermittent and/or continuous rate of responding, the behavioral model (e.g., positive behavioral support) also provides for an understanding of functional behavior that may explain some of the processes or reasons underlying the humor, stress, and health status relationship. Thus, in partial accord with other theories, we further speculate that the behavioral purposes underlying humor and laughter may be viewed as multifunctional; that is, the payoff for both humor use and laughter serves several functions or purposes, including, to obtain attention (e.g., social reinforcement), to engage in a needed activity (social activity) or to obtain a tangible (e.g., money), to escape or avoid a demand or instructional cue (e.g., social threat), and to decrease or increase sensory over/under load, respectively (e.g., tension reduction; see e.g., Durand, 1999).[13] While these assumed behavioral functions have yet to be tested in relation to humor, at least to our knowledge, and although some of these have been alluded to by other scholars in a non-behavioral sense (e.g., Martin, 2002), the functional model deserves further scrutiny (see Martin & Pear, 2007, O'Neill et al., 1997 and Luiselli & Cameron, 1998 for related behavioral examples of the functional model).

More research is also warranted for both Pavlovian (e.g., laughter as an unconditioned or conditioned reflex to a conditioned/unconditioned stimulus) and social-cognitive models (e.g., humor self-efficacy, planned behavior). For example, a vast body of research suggests that self-efficacy is linked to health, health behavior, and adjustment (see e.g., Bandura, 1997, p. 259).[14] One intriguing question concerns the role of humor and

---

[13] O'Neill et al. (1997) and others expand on these functions. For example, in relation to problem behavior, O'Neill et al. suggest that there are 6 possible functions of behavior that include, (1) *Positive Automatic Reinforcement* (i.e., to obtain internal stimulation), (2) *Positive Reinforcement: Social* (i.e., to obtain attention), (3) *Positive Reinforcement: Tangible/Activity* (i.e., to engage in an activity or obtain a tangible), (4) *Negative Automatic Reinforcement* (i.e., to escape/avoid internal stimulation), (5) *Negative Reinforcement: Escape Motivated Social* (i.e., to escape/avoid attention), and (6) *Negative Reinforcement: Escape Motivated Task* (i.e., to escape/avoid tasks, activities).

[14] Grossman makes further reference to social learning in relation to humor and therapy:

It may also be that some jokes that are reported as favourites are more a function of social learning and may reflect problems of cultural groups, not

laughter efficacy in confronting the demands of various stressors. Given the variability and relative instability of humor use and response, it is not clear how confident (i.e., self-efficacy) some individuals are in their use of humor, in their use of humor to combat stress, in their beliefs about the benefits of humor (i.e., outcome expectations), in their ability to learn the technical aspects of humor generation from others through for example, modeling and observational learning, as well as in their ability to self-regulate or control their use of humor (e.g., *mindful* versus *mindless* humor use), including its perception.[15] In any case, behavioral models (i.e., behavioral functions, social-cognitive theory) propose that individuals may use humor and laughter (a) to escape/avoid stress, (b) to decrease/increase sensory over/underload, (c) to obtain attention which may have health enhancing effects, (d) as a needed social activity or to receive a tangible, (e) reflexively, and/or (f) to self-regulate their use of humor in response to stress. All of these are vital and competitive hypotheses.[16]

SUMMARY OF THEORETICAL EXPLANATIONS FOR THE BENEFITS OF HUMOR

In summary, though not fully inclusive, four general models may help to explain the role of humor in coping.[17,18] The arousal model (e.g., Berlyne, 1972; Freud, 1905, 1928) suggests that humor helps to relieve

---

specifically those of the individual who repeats them. This does not, however, preclude the possibility that the social problem is not a troublesome one of the patient. In addition, some people's problems may be so complex that many kinds of jokes reflect some aspect of their personality.

[15] We are currently testing such a model.

[16] See Epstein and Joker (2007) for a discussion of a *Threshold Theory of the Humor Response*. Their discussion also provides further insight into behaviorism, humor, and laughter.

[17] See Vollrath (2001) and Friedman (2008) for a discussion of the various mechanisms and pathways linking personality to health (e.g., stress appraisal, genetics, health behavior). These models may also hold some credence in explaining the processes linking trait humor to health and illness.

[18] We speculate on the role of these models for our study in the Conclusion section.

excessive levels of psychological/physical tension or arousal. The incongruity models (e.g., Koestler, 1964) provide us with a cognitive-perceptual understanding of the role of expectancy violation as a precursor of, for example laughter, which may subsequently influence the experience of positive affect. Superiority models (e.g., Gruner, 1997; Levine, 1977) suggest that feelings of competence and mastery over the environment result from the disparagement of others or one self. The last model suggests that humor and laughter may serve several behavioral functions (e.g., escape, avoidance). Indeed, the behavioral model appears to share some features with the arousal (e.g., sensory overload reduction) and superiority perspectives, it also distinguishes itself from the other perspectives by its focus on the objective external determinants and outputs (i.e., excesses and deficits) of behavior, as well as the many functions to which humorous behavior may be linked. Social-cognitive and Pavlovian models may also be of use in furthering our understanding of humor although such models may lack the richness in description and subjectivity, a quality in part, inherent to the humor experience. However, what the general behavioral model lacks in description, it more than makes up for in sound empirical support in relation to many of its hypotheses (see e.g., *The Journal of Applied Behavior Analysis*). We next examine how humor and laughter have been measured to help test some of these theoretical predictions.

MEASUREMENT OF HUMOR AND LAUGHTER

A patient says to his therapist, 'Thank you doctor for curing my kleptomania. Is there anything I can ever do to repay you?'

The doctor replies, 'Well…. If you ever relapse, could you pick up a video recorder for my son?'

- Dunkelblau (1987, p. 309)

Even though many definitions of humor exist, it is generally accepted that humor "represents a rather complex higher-order cognitive-emotional process, whereas laughter is a reflex-like physiological-behavioral response" (Lefcourt & Martin, 1986, p. 31). Expanding on this, Martin (2007) suggests that,

> humor is a broad term that refers to anything that people say or do that is perceived as funny and tends to make others laugh, as well as the mental processes that go into both creating and perceiving such an amusing stimulus, and also the affective response involved in the enjoyment of it (p. 5).

Thus, four elements or components help to define the humor experience, the social context, a cognitive-perceptual process, an emotional response, as well as the vocal-behavioral expression of laughter (Martin, 2007, p. 5). Although the humor concept has evolved into an "umbrella term for all humor and laughter-related phenomenon" (Martin, 2003), several other authors have proposed more specific definitions and taxonomies (see Ruch, 1998, p. 6 for a discussion of several taxonomies related to humor; see also Hehl & Ruch, 1985, Levine & Rakusin, 1958, and Moody, 1978). For example, in an early study comparing the sense of humor of college students to that of psychiatric patients, Levine and Rakusin (1959) loosely defined it in both active (making others laugh) and reactive (appreciation – readiness to laugh) terms. Eysenck (1972) has also argued that humor should be conceptualized and studied as a typology. For instance, Eysenck described sense of humor in three ways or *senses*: (1) *The Conformist Sense:* A person with a good sense of humor laughs at similar things that others laugh at; (2) *The Quantitative Sense:* Refers to the person who is amused easily and laughs to a great extent; and (3) *The Productive Sense:* Refers to the person who tells jokes and amuses others.

In contrast, Moody (1978) has proposed a broader typology, describing humor in six ways (egocentric to general types). These types are: (1) *The-He-Realizes-How-Funny-I-Am Sense:* A person has a good sense of humor when another person can get that person to laugh whenever he or she wants to; (2) *The Conventional Sense:* This type refers to the degree that a person laughs at things others laugh at; (3) *The Life-of-the-Party Sense:* This person is one who is skilled at telling an array of jokes and funny stories and making others laugh; (4) *The Creative Sense:* Refers to the ability to create humor, and/or other funny things; (5) *The Good-Sport Sense:* Generally, this sense refers to the ability to laugh at oneself or "to take a joke"; and (6) *The Cosmic Perspective:* Refers to the person who sees him- or herself and others in a detached light. Such a person views life humorously, yet remains in positive contact with others and the events surrounding him or her. This type has the most therapeutic relevance. As this discussion alludes to, the effects of humor and laughter on stress and health are determined in part by the different ways in which mirthfulness has been operationalized.

One construct issue that appears to be a source of confusion or bewilderment for some researchers, concerns the number and types of humor and laughter measures in use. For example, according to Ruch (1998), the following eight types of humor measures have been utilized since the early 1970s: (1) informal surveys, joke telling techniques, diary methods (e.g., Humor Initiation Scales; Bell, McGree, & Duffey, 1986); (2) joke and cartoon tests (e.g., 3 WD Humor Test; Ruch,1992); (3) questionnaires, self-report scales (e.g., Situational Humor Response Questionnaire, Martin & Lefcourt, 1984); (4) peer-reports (e.g., Test of the Sociometry of Humor; Ziv, 1984); (5) state measures (e.g., State-Trait Cheerfulness Inventory-State part; Ruch, Kohler, & van Thriel, 1997); (6) humor tests for children (e.g., Children's Mirth Response Test; Zigler, Levine, & Gould, 1966); (7) humor scales in general instruments (e.g., COPE; Carver, Scheier, & Weintraub, 1989); and (8) miscellaneous and unclassified tests of humor (e.g., Wittiness Questionnaire; Turner, 1980). While particularly impressive in their sophistication and scope, it is important to note that many of these scales assess different aspects of the humor experience such as humor style (e.g., Martin et al., 2003), appreciation (e.g., Herzog & Strevey, 2008), initiation, expression, production, or creation (i.e., Zweyer, Velker, & Ruch, 2004), coping humor (e.g., Martin, 1996), joke preference (e.g., Mindess et al.), humor motivation and communication (e.g., Feingold & Mazzella, 1993), personal liking of humor (e.g., Svebak, 1974), comprehension or getting the joke (Semrud-Clikeman, & Glass, 2008), and perception or sensitivity to humorous cues (e.g., Bonanno & Jost, 2006; Cann & Etzel, 2008; Eysenck, 1972; Hehl & Ruch, 1985; Levine & Rakusin, 1959; Martin et al., 2003; Moody, 1978; Svebak, 1974, 1996). As might be expected, the intercorrelations amongst these measures have often been found to be moderate in size but stronger than in relation to various nonhumor related constructs (e.g., physical health). One well known and widely used questionnaire in particular, the *Situational Humor Response Questionnaire* (SHRQ: Caldwell, Cervone, & Rubin, 2008; Martin, 1996; Martin & Lefcourt, 1984), is a case in point.

The SHRQ is a 21-item habit related questionnaire constructed to measure individual differences or behavioral tendencies in humorous responding (smiles, laughs) across a range of situations (see Martin, 1996 and Ruch & Deckers, 1993). Its psychometric characteristics are respectable with reported estimates of internal consistency ranging from .70 to .83 and a one-month test-retest reliability of .70. The SHRQ has also been found to be free of any social desirability bias (Martin & Lefcourt, 1984; see also Martin, 1996 and Ruch & Deckers, 1993) and has been linked to other measures of humor (e.g., affiliative and self-enhancing humor; Martin et al., 2003), as well as the frequency and length of spontaneous laughter, peer ratings of humor and laughter, humorous monologues tested in a laboratory setting (see Martin, 2003 for a brief review of the SHRQ), and personality characteristics such as psychoticism and extraversion (e.g., Ruch & Deckers, 1993), in addition to morale, perceived health (Simon, 1988), body preoccupation, health utilization behavior (Kuiper & Nicholl, 2004), immune function (Martin & Dobbin, 1988), depression, self-esteem (Kuiper & Borowicz-Siibenik, 2005), burnout (Fry, 1995), general health (Simon, 1988), and mood disturbance (Martin & Lefcourt, 1984; see also Martin, 1996). According to Martin (1996), in a review of the SHRQ and the Coping Humor Scale, the SHRQ has been found to moderate or buffer the impact of stress on various mood and health related states such as depression, mood balance, positive affect, and indirectly, immune function. Further, those who laugh and smile across a variety of situations tend to use more effective and realistic cognitive appraisals, have a healthier self-concept and high self-esteem, use a variety of defense mechanisms, report greater levels of optimism and feelings of coherence, as well as higher levels of intimacy in social interaction.

For the researcher and clinician interested in using the SHRQ as part of one's assessment or survey package, the current version may not be appropriate for some test situations. For example, despite its impressive psychometric characteristics and modest scope, the SHRQ requires the participant to respond to several lengthy, pleasant and unpleasant situations with unusually long response options. These options also vary across the questionnaire. For example, the stem for question 9 reads, "If you were watching a movie or T.V. program with some friends and you found one scene particularly funny, but no one else appeared to find it humorous, how would you have reacted most commonly?" Using a Guttman-like set of response options, the participant would then respond to a multiple choice scale ranging from a – "I would have concluded that I must have misunderstood something or that it wasn't really funny" to, e – "I would have laughed heartily." Thus, a less cognitively complex and time consuming measure would be useful in, for example, mass testing situations, or in other contexts where time is of the essence. As Marshall et al. (1994) point out, researchers must often make a choice between brevity and comprehensiveness in the selection of their measures. The same case can be made for the measurement of humor. In this case, we examine the SHRQ.

Given these limitations and to complement the full measure as a potential alternative in certain situations, three studies are reported herein detailing the development of a brief 12-item version of the SHRQ. In study 1, the items were selected and subjected to a principal components analysis in order to assess its construct validity. We also examined its correlates and tested for gender differences in responding. In both studies 1 and 2, the brief version was compared to the full 21-item version. Further, in study 2, the data were subjected to a principal components analysis, as well as a moderated regression analysis. Within the context of stress moderation (Moderator Model; see Figure 1b), it was predicted that both the brief and extended versions would be found to buffer the relationship between perceived stress and health; that is, participants who self-report as responding with humor and laughter across a wide variety of situations and when under high stress, would also report fewer health concerns. As Figure 1b indicates, humor, acting as an antecedent moderator variable, is assumed to influence the magnitude and direction of the relationship between stress and illness or health. While the moderator models focuses on the conditions in which humor may impact stress and health or illness, the mediator model (Figure 1c) helps us to understand the process underlying humors impact on illness or health.[19] The Direct Effects Model (Figure 1a) proposes a one-to-one relationship between the predictor or independent variable (e.g., humor) and the criterion or dependent variable (e.g., health). We focus on the direct effects and moderator models.

Last, in study 3 we correlated the two SHRQs with a host of personality (Five-Factor Model), coping (trait based), daily stress, health (life satisfaction, happiness, affect, symptomatology, general health, life expectancy), and demographic variables. This was followed by a series of multiple regression analyses using both SHRQs as the criteria. To further assess its construct validity, the SHRQs were once again subjected to a principal components analysis. And last, we ran several analyses to determine if both SHRQs discriminated between the sexes on a number of humor and nonhumor related variables.

(a)

---

[19] The moderator model arose, in part, from the often-found low correlations between life stress and illness. It was thus thought that certain antecedent variables or groups experienced greater or lesser rates of illness and stress. For example, hardy individuals have been found to experience lower rates of stress and illness relative to those less hardy (e.g., Kobasa, 1979; see also Lefcourt & Thomas, 1998).

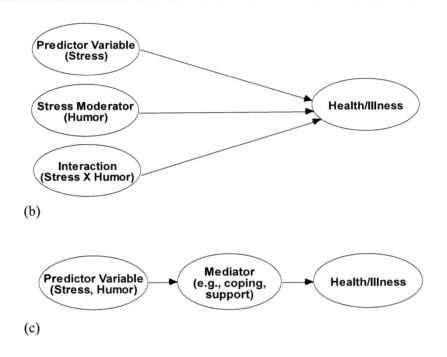

(b)

(c)

Figure 1. Research models: Main/Direct, Moderator, Mediator.

(a): Main/Direct Effects Model.

(b): Stress Moderator Model.

(c): Mediator Model.

Chapter 2

STUDY 1

METHOD

Participants and Procedure

Twenty-five male and 65 female (N = 90) first year psychology students with a mean age of 20.17 years (SD = 2.90) participated in this study. Data collection took place in small groups.[20]

Questionnaires were randomized to help offset potential order effects. Upon completion of the test, participants then rated the tracks. Participants were tested in groups over a two-week period.

---

[20] A smaller version of this data set was used in a study conducted by Korotkov (1991). The present study and the 1991 study differ in several respects. For example, in Korotkov, an additional humor measure, the Conformist Humor Rating Measure (see below) was not included; the stress and health measures described herein were excluded (not available) as well. Further, the results reported in our research were analyzed in greater depth and with different analytic techniques (e.g., multiple regression). And last, the SHQ measure used in Korotkov differs from the one used herein.

Measures

The following measures were administered to all participants:

1) *The Situational Humor Response Questionnaire* (SHRQ; Martin & Lefcourt, 1984). As discussed in the introduction, this 21-item scale defines sense of humor "as the frequency with which the individual smiles, laughs, or otherwise displays amusement in a variety of situations." The 21-items are summed to give a total score. Those with high scores tend to laugh and smile in a variety of situations.

2) *Humor Initiation and Responsiveness Measure* (HIRM; Bell, McGhee, & Duffy, 1986; as cited in Nahemour, McCluskey-Fawcett, & McGhee, 1986). This 7-item scale assesses both humor initiation and response. Of the seven items, six pertain to different aspects of humor initiation. For instance, "How often do you use puns in an attempt to create your own humor?" The items on this index are summed to give a total initiation score, with high scores indicating higher levels of humor production. The seventh item deals with humor responsiveness (HR): "How often do you have a strong belly laugh of the type that lasts 5 seconds or more?" For this item, higher ratings reflect greater levels of laughter.

3) *The Sense of Humor Questionnaire* (SHQ; Svebak, 1974). This 21-item measure assumes that humor production and appreciation consists of three separate qualities: (i) Metamessage Sensitivity – reflects the ability to perceive various humorous cues in the environment. A sample item is "I must admit that I am usually slow at noticing humorous points or catching onto jokes"; (ii) Personal Liking of Humor – refers to the subjective liking and enjoyment of humor (e.g., "A humorist is typically perceived by others as a person who lacks the courage of this convictions"); and (iii) Emotional Permissivness – refers to the extent to which an individual expresses his or her emotions (e.g., "If I have an unrestrained fit of laughter, I often have misgivings that others

thought I was a bit of an exhibitionist"). All three measures are scored on a four-point scale ranging from 1 = *Strongly Disagree* to 4 = *Strongly Agree*.[21] High scores on each of the scales indicates higher levels of sensitivity, liking, and permissiveness.

4) *The Coping Humor Scale* (CHS; Martin & Lefcourt, 1983). The CHS is a seven-item measure that directly assesses the extent to which participants report having used humor as a coping device against stress. A sample item is "It has been my experience that humor is a very effective way of coping with problems." Participants are required to rate the extent of agreement or disagreement on a four-point Likert-type scale from 1 = *Strongly Disagree* to 4 = *Strongly Agree*. To obtain a total score, all items were reverse scored prior to summing. High scores reflect a greater tendency to use humor as a coping strategy.

5) *Conformist Humor Rating Measure.* In contrast to the other humor questionnaires, a behavioral or conformist measure of humor appreciation/funniness was included. In constructing this measure, two judges (one male, one female) *initially* rated the degree of mirth in 46 randomized auditory comedy tracks on a seven-point index from 1 = *Not Funny at All* to 7 = *Very Funny*. For ethical reasons, sexual, ethnic, sexist, or sick humor tracks were excluded. From this, the top (scored) 19 auditory tracks were selected and randomized. Each track varied by time and artist (e.g., Robin Williams, Steve Martin). In the actual testing sessions, participants were required to rate each track on the forementioned seven-point

---

[21] Because of concerns surrounding the internal consistency of the SHQ, three items from each of its subscales (i.e., Personal Liking of Humor, Metamessage Sensitivity, and Emotional Permissiveness) with the highest corrected item-total correlations were selected and subsequently combined into a composite measure (alpha = .60: see Svebak, Martin, & Holmen, 2004). Examination of the correlation matrix (see Table 1of study 1) found that, in line with previous studies (e.g., Svebak, Götestam, & Jensen, 2004), this 9-item SHQ measure tended to be more strongly correlated with the other humor variables and less so with the stress and symptom measures. Thus, for the purposes of this research, this 9-item scale appears to reflect a broad personality construct related to the sense of humor (i.e., emotional expression, liking, and sensitivity to humorous cues).

scale. Total time for presentation of the tracks was approximately 45 minutes. The cassette tape was played on a prosonic fm/sw/am detachable component system, d2-way speaker system. Alpha was found to be .87 (overall mean = 82.17, SD = 14.65). Higher self-reported scores indicate greater levels of humor appreciation/ funniness or responsiveness.

6) *The Daily Hassles Scale* (DHS; Kanner, Coyne, Schaefer, & Lazarus, 1981). The DHS is a 117-item inventory containing various minor nuisances, which participants respond to based on the past month. Each participant was required to rate the items on a three-point scale ranging from, 1 = *Somewhat Severe* to 3 = *Extremely Severe*. The DHS frequency score (DHF) was used in all analyses. Items on this measure pertain to the following life areas: work, family, finances, environment, social activities, and health. As some researchers have expressed concern over several health-related items within the DHS, nine such items were removed (i.e., "trouble relaxing," "trouble making decisions," "physical illness," "side effects of medication," "sexual problems that result from physical problems," "difficulties seeing or hearing," "not enough personal energy," "loneliness," "nightmares"). High scores reflect greater levels of daily stress experienced over the past month.

7) *The Health Opinion Survey* (HOS; MacMillan, 1957). This abridged 10-item symptomatology inventory was originally designed to screen for persons in the general population who suffer from excessive preoccupation with their health. Participants are required to rate each item on a 1 (*Never*) to 5 (*Nearly all the time*) scale to indicate the degree to which a symptom was experienced during the past two weeks. All indicators are summed to yield a total symptomatology score. Examples of such items include "How often have you had trouble getting to sleep or staying asleep," and "How often have you been troubled by a headache or pain in the head?"

RESULTS

Overview

Descriptive statistics were first calculated. Next, 12-items were selected to comprise a brief version of the SHRQ. Follow-up principal components analysis using the humor and nonhumor measures provided preliminary support for the construct validity of the 12-item SHRQ. Both versions of the SHRQ were also found to be predicted by the Humor Initiation and Response Measure as well as the Coping Humor Scale. Both SHRQs were highly correlated with each other. No sex differences were found with either SHRQ measure. Overall, the analyses in Study 1 suggest that the 12-item SHRQ parallels the 21-item measure.

Chart 2. Means, standard deviations, and intercorrelations for each of the study1 variables (N = 90)

Variables	1	2	3	4	5	6	7	8	9
1. Sex	-								
2. S-12	.04	-							
3. S-21	.03	.94**	-						
4. CR	-.25*	.44**	.50**	-					
5. HIRM	-.14	.39**	.43**	.36**	-				
6. SHQ	-.06	.30**	.28**	.26*	.42**	-			
7. CHS	.10	.23*	.26*	-.08	.22*	.18†	-		
8. DHF	.25*	-.04	-.04	.06	-.02	-.15	.06	-	
9. HOS	.31**	-.09	-.07	-.07	-.03	-.24*	.03	.45**	-
Mean	-	34.33	61.66	82.17	18.62	28.14	19.83	26.85	21.70
SD	-	5.78	9.08	14.65	4.90	3.66	2.84	14.28	6.21

Note: S-12 = 12-item SHRQ, S-21 = 21-item SHRQ, CR = humor ratings of audio tracks, HIRM = Humor Initiation and Response Measure, SHQ = Sense of Humor Questionnaire, CHS = Coping Humor Scale, DHF = Daily Hassles Frequency, HOS = Health Opinion Survey, SD = Standard Deviation.
  †$p < .10$ *$p < .05$ **$p < .01$.

Item Selection and Descriptive Statistics

To develop a brief measure of the SHRQ that would take an average person approximately half the time to complete, nine situational items from the original measure were first selected based on the highest corrected item-total correlations. In keeping with the theoretical orientation of the original instrument, the three nonsituational questions from the SHRQ were also included. In sum, the 12-items selected for use were: 3, 7, 8, 9, 10, 11, 12, 14, 15, 19, 20, and 21 (see Martin & Lefcourt, 1984 for a copy of the 21-item questionnaire).[22] The 12-item version was found to have an alpha of .72 (men = .80, women = .70), well within previous research estimates of the 21-item scale (e.g., Lefcourt & Martin, 1983). The alpha coefficient for the 21-item measure was found to be .78 (men = .84, women = .75). The means, SDs, as well as a correlation matrix for each of the variables can be found in Chart 2. As Chart 2 indicates, the 12-item measure was found to be highly correlated with the 21-item measure (r = .94).

Construct Validity

To provide a more stringent test of the SHRQ's divergent and convergent validity, two principal components analyses (PCA) with promax rotations were carried out using each of the humor, stress, and health measures. For each analysis, three components emerged. When the 12-item SHRQ was used, the following three component structure was found (.40 loading cut-off): (1) the humor response item (λ = .94), the 12-item SHRQ (λ = .69), the Humor Initiation Measure (λ = .58); (2) daily

---

[22] With the exception of items 19, 20, and 21, the remaining situational items are scored in a positive direction. Item 19 reflects the extent to which the individual prefers other individuals with a similar sense of humor. Item 20 is a nonsituational question that requests the respondent to indicate the frequency with which they laugh when compared to an average individual. Item 21 assesses the extent to which the person is consistent from situation to situation in their use of humor. See Lefcourt and Martin (1986, p. 23; see also Martin & Lefcourt, 1984) for a more detailed discussion concerning these items.

hassles frequency (λ = .85), the Health Opinion Survey (λ = .85); and (3) the Coping Humor Scale (λ = .94), and the Sense of Humor Questionnaire (λ = .43). The total variance accounted for by this solution was 67.64 %. Similarly, when the 21-item SHRQ was used in place of the 12-item SHRQ, the following components emerged: (1) the humor response item (λ = .96), the 21-item SHRQ (λ = .73), the Humor Initiation Measure (λ = .56); (2) daily hassles frequency (λ = .85), the Health Opinion Survey (λ = .85); and (3) the Coping Humor Scale (λ = .94), and the Sense of Humor Questionnaire (λ = .45). The total variance accounted for by these components was 68.46 %.

SHRQ Correlates

Two stepwise multiple regression analyses were next carried out using the 12- and 21-item SHRQ versions as separate criterion variables. Each of the humor, hassles, and symptomatology scales were entered as predictors into each regression equation. The results from both analyses were similar although the percentage of variance accounted for in the criteria differed somewhat. When the 12-item SHRQ served as the criterion, the humor response item (β = .44, p < .001) and the Coping Humor Scale (β = .27, p < .01) were found to be significant (R^2 = .25). Similarly, when the 21-item SHRQ was the criterion variable, the humor response item (β = .50, p < .001), and the Coping Humor Scale (β = .31, p < .001) were once again found to be statistically significant (R^2 = .33).

Sex Differences

The main effects of sex, humor (12- and 21-item SHRQ), and their interactions were also examined in relation to each of the humor and health variables. No significant main effects or interactions were found (p > .10) suggesting that the two versions were responded to similarly by both men and women. Sex was also uncorrelated with either of the SHRQs (see Chart 2).

DISCUSSION

With few notable exceptions, the results indicated that the 12-item SHRQ performed in a manner similar to that of the 21-item measure. As expected, both measures diverged from the stress and health scales while converging with other measures of humor and laughter. The 12-item SHRQ was also highly correlated with the 21-item SHRQ and possessed an acceptable level of internal consistency comparable to previous studies. Lastly, no sex differences were found for either of the two versions.

The purpose of study 2 was to validate these findings with a larger sample and with different measures of stress and health. Given its reported health enhancing effects as a personality measure, we also tested a direct effects model of humor (main effects: 12- and 21-item SHRQ) on health as well as stress moderator model.

Chapter 3

STUDY 2

METHOD

Participants, Measures, and Procedure

Data were collected from 541 university students (n_{men} = 207, n_{women} = 334, 2 participants did not indicate sex) with a mean age of 20.45 years (SD = 4.13).[23] As in the first study, the following measures were administered to participants in a classroom setting: a demographics questionnaire (i.e., sex, age), the 21-item SHRQ (Martin & Lefcourt, 1984), and a one-item question from the HIRM (i.e., "How often do you have a strong belly laugh of the type that last 5 seconds or more": Nahemow et al., 1986). The other measures were unique to Study 2 and included the following:

1) *Daily Hassles* (DHS-56; see e.g., Delongis, Folkman, & Lazarus, 1988). To measure daily stress, a 56-item measure was administered to participants. Based in part on Delongis et al.

---

[23] A small subset of these variables were analyzed and recently published in Korotkov (2010a and 2010b). In Korotkov (2010a and b), optimism, humor, happiness, and vigor were not incorporated into the study; similarly, one of the stress measures' also differed (i.e., DHS-56 vs. DHS-85). Further, distinct hypotheses, study rationale, and analyses, differed as well.

(1988), each participant rated the extent to which 56 hassles (e.g., social, academic) were experienced during the past month. Participants used a four-point rating scale for each item (0 = *None, not applicable* to 3 = *A great deal*). High scores reflect more daily stress.

2) *The Inventory of College Students' Recent Life Experiences* (ICRLES-17: Korotkov, 2010a, 2010b; see Kohn, Lafreniere, & Gurevich, 1990 for the full measure). A second measure of daily stress was based on a 17-item abbreviated version of Kohn et al.'s 40-item student hassles measure (e.g., *time pressures*). Each participant responded to the items using a four-point scale ranging from 1 = *Not at all part of my life* to 4 = *Very much part of my life.* All items are summed to form a total stress score. As with the DHS-56, high scores indicate greater levels of stress (during the past four weeks).

3) *Short-form Perceived Stress Scale* (PSS; Cohen & Williamson, 1988). A third measure of stress was also included as part of the test battery. The short version of the PSS is comprised of four-items (e.g., "In the last month, how often have you felt that things were going your way?") for which participants rate their perceived stress levels using a five-point scale that ranges from 0 = *Never* to 4 = *Very often*. All items are summed to form a total perceived stress score (i.e., high scores = greater perceived stress).

4) *The Memorial University of Newfoundland Scale of Happiness* (MUNSH; Kozma, Stones, & McNeil, 1991). The MUNSH is a 24-item measure designed to assess levels of trait happiness. Each of the items (e.g., "The things I do are as interesting to me as they ever were") are rated on the following three-point scale: 1 (?), 0 (No), and 2 (Yes). High scores reflect greater levels of happiness.

5) *The Memorial University of Newfoundland Mood Scale* (MUMS; see Kozma et al., 1991 and McNeil, 1987). A 23-item version of the MUMS was used to measure positive (eight items; e.g., "pleasant") and negative (eight items; e.g., "downhearted") mood, as well as vigor (seven items; e.g., "peppy"). Each adjective was

rated on the following three-point scale: 2 = *Yes, I did feel*, 1 = *Cannot decide*, and 0 = *No, I did not feel*. High scores on each measure reflects higher self-reported feelings of positive and negative mood, and vigor.

6) *Dispositional Optimism* (OPT; see e.g., Scheier & Carver, 1987). Optimism was measured by a two-item scale adapted from Scheier and Carver (1987). Both items are rated on a five-point scale from 0 = *Strongly Disagree* to 4 = *Strongly Agree*.

7) *Extraversion* (EXT). Based on Table 1 of McCrae and Costa (1985; see Korotkov, 2010a, 2010b), a ten-item, nine-point bipolar adjective checklist was used to measure extraversion (e.g., 1 = "Talkative" to 9 = "Quiet"). High scores on the measure reflect a tendency towards extraversion. The items include "aloof-friendly," "affectionate-reserved," "sociable-retiring," "quiet-talkative," "loner-joiner," "inhibited-spontaneous," "unemotional-emotional," "fun-loving-sober," and "impulse ridden-not impulse ridden."

8) *Memorial University of Newfoundland Symptomatology Scale* (MUSS; Korotkov, 2000). To measure symptomatology, a ten-item perceived symptomatology scale was administered to participants. Each of the symptoms (e.g., "Hands trembling," "Headache") is rated on a five-point scale that ranges from 0 (*Not at all*) to 4 (*Extremely*). The items include, hands trembling, dizziness, heart pounding or racing, poor appetite, feeling low in energy, felt weak all over, muscle cramps, faintness, headache, and constant fatigue. Participants are to respond to each item based on the past two weeks. All items are summed to form a total symptom score (i.e., high scores = higher levels of symptomatology).

RESULTS

Overview

Descriptive statistics were first calculated. As in Study 1, the 12-item SHRQ was strongly correlated with its parent measure. A second set of principal components analyses with both the humor and nonhumor measures suggested that the SHRQ measures diverged from the stress and health related measures. The SHRQs loaded on the component with the other "positive" personality variables. Stepwise regression analyses further suggested that the SHRQs were predicted by humor, vigor, and the personality variables. Further analyses found no significant differences between the male and female participants on either of the SHRQs. Last, a series of stress moderator analyses using moderated multiple regression yielded a number of significant interactions for both SHRQ measures, suggesting that humor/laughter was a stress bufferer. Generally, these findings provide further support for the 12-item SHRQ as a brief measure of this valuable humor construct.

Descriptive Statistics

The means, SDs, as well as a correlation matrix for each of the variables can be found in Chart 3. As Chart 3 indicates, the SHRQs were strongly correlated with each other ($r = .92$), with the personality and mood measures, but less so with the stress and symptom measures. The alpha coefficient for the 12-item version was found to be .69 (men = .67, women = .71) and .78 (men = .78, women = .79) for the full measure. Despite these variations, as a following section will detail, no sex differences were found.

Construct Validity

To determine whether both versions of the SHRQ would load on the same component as the personality and positive mood measures but diverge from the stress, negative mood, and symptom measures, two PCAs with promax rotations were used. With the exception of the Memorial University Scale of Happiness, the results generally supported these expectations. In both analyses, two components were found. When the 12-

item SHRQ was used, the Inventory of College Students Recent Life Experiences ($\lambda = .91$), the 56-item daily hassles measure ($\lambda = .85$), the Memorial University Symptom Scale ($\lambda = .81$), the Perceived Stress Scale ($\lambda = .79$), the Memorial University of Newfoundland Scale of Happiness ($\lambda = -.67$), negative mood ($\lambda = .66$), and positive mood ($\lambda = -.42$) all loaded on the first component with $\lambda = .40$ as the cut-off. The second component was comprised of the one-item humor measure ($\lambda = .75$), the 12-item SHRQ ($\lambda = .73$), extraversion ($\lambda = .73$), vigor ($\lambda = .56$), positive mood ($\lambda = .56$), and optimism ($\lambda = .41$). A similar pattern was found when the 21-item SHRQ was used. Component 1 was comprised of the following variables: the 17-item Inventory of College Students Recent Life Experiences ($\lambda = .91$), the 56-item daily hassles scale ($\lambda = .85$), the Memorial University Symptom Scale ($\lambda = .81$), the Perceived Stress Scale ($\lambda = .79$), the Memorial University of Newfoundland Scale of Happiness ($\lambda = -.66$), negative mood ($\lambda = .66$), and positive mood ($\lambda = -.41$). As in the first analysis, the following variables loaded on component 2: the 21-item SHRQ ($\lambda = .75$), extraversion ($\lambda = .74$), the humor response item ($\lambda = .73$), positive mood ($\lambda = .57$), vigor ($\lambda = .57$), and optimism ($\lambda = .43$).

SHRQ Correlates

A set of stepwise multiple regression analyses were once again run to assess the independent correlates of both SHRQs. Both humor measures were regressed on the humor, personality, stress, symptom, and mood variables. In the first analysis, the humor response item ($\beta = .29, p < .001$), optimism ($\beta = .18, p < .001$), extraversion ($\beta = .16, p < .001$), and vigor ($\beta = .11, p < .05$) predicted the 12-item SHRQ ($R^2 = .26$). When the 21-item SHRQ was used, the same variables predicted the criterion ($R^2 = .28$): the humor response item ($\beta = .26, p < .001$), optimism ($\beta = .20, p < .001$), extraversion ($\beta = .19, p < .001$), and vigor ($\beta = .12, p < .05$).

Chart 3. Means, standard deviations, and intercorrelations for each of the study 2 variables

Variables	1	2	3	4	5	6	7	8	9	10	11	12	13	14
1. Sex	-													
2. Age	-.03	-												
3. S-12	-.01	-.07	-											
4. S-21	-.01	-.11*	.92**	-										
5. MUNSH	-.15**	.06	.23**	.26**	-									
6. EXT	.10*	-.12**	.36**	.38**	.27**	-								
7. OPT	-.10*	.09*	.33**	.36**	.56**	.29**	-							
8. DHS-56	.02	-.01	-.07	-.09†	-.35**	-.07	-.25**	-						
9. ICSRLE	.05	-.17**	-.16**	-.17*	-.51**	-.10*	-.39**	.61**	-					
10. PSS	.14**	-.11*	-.23**	-.22**	-.64**	-.17**	-.49**	.45**	.62**	-				
11. MUSS	.23**	-.09*	-.16**	-.15**	-.45**	-.11*	-.37**	.47**	.51**	.51**	-			
12. NMD	.09*	-.10*	-.21**	-.22**	-.62**	-.24**	-.43**	.32**	.52**	.61**	.50**	-		
13. PMD	-.06	.07†	.30**	.33**	.65**	.38**	.52**	-.25**	-.42**	-.59**	-.40**	-.57**	-	
14. Vigor	-.20**	.04	.31**	.33**	.55**	.36**	.47**	-.19**	-.35**	-.52**	-.47**	-.46**	.77**	-
Mean	-	-	33.12	60.20	8.51	65.01	7.06	43.22	21.59	6.88	8.31	18.00	27.34	25.25
SD	-	-	5.39	9.10	9.59	11.67	1.88	20.34	8.25	2.97	6.60	5.52	5.24	5.38

Note: S-12 = 12-item SHRQ, S-21 = 21-item SHRQ, MUNSH = Memorial University of Newfoundland Scale of Happiness (MUNSH), EXT = Extraversion, OPT = Optimism, DHS-56 = Daily Hassles Scale – 56, ICSRLE = Inventory of College Students Recent Life Experiences (ICSRLE-17), PSS = Perceived Stress Scale, MUSS = Memorial University of Newfoundland Symptom Scale, NMD = Negative Mood, PMD = Positive Mood, SD = Standard Deviation.

† $p < .10$ * $p < .05$ ** $p < .01$

Sex Differences

Tests of the main effects of sex, humor (SHRQ), and their interactions in relation to each of the stress, symptom, mood, personality, and humor measures were again conducted. Despite the larger sample size, no significant differences on any of the variables were found between men and women (all $ps > .05$). In addition, sex was not correlated with either the brief or full versions of the SHRQ (see Chart 3).

Stress Moderation

Given that previous studies suggest that the SHRQ may demonstrate stress and health effects (e.g, Martin, 1996), we next tested whether one or both versions would either directly predict (i.e., main effects) or interact with stress to impact the latter's relationship with physical symptomatology, negative mood, positive mood, and vigor. To assess this, the 56-item daily hassles scale, the 17-item Inventory of College Students Recent Life Experiences, and the Perceived Stress Scale served as the stressor predictor variables in three separate sets of moderated multiple regression analyses, respectively. As recommended by several researchers (e.g., Frazier, Tix, & Baron, 2004), each of the stress and humor variables were first centered prior to the main analyses. In each analysis, hierarchical multiple regression was used with the demographic variables (sex and age of participant) entered on step one, the stress deviation score variable entered at step two, the humor deviation scores entered at step 3, and last, the stress by humor product-term deviation scores at step four. A significant interaction indicates a stress moderation effect (ΔR^2).[24]

The Daily Hassles-56

When the full SHRQ scale was first analyzed, significant interaction effects were found with respect to both vigor ($\Delta R^2 = .01$, $p < .05$) and

---

[24] To simplify interpretation, the main effects for the other variables (e.g., stress) are not reported here.

symptomatology ($\Delta R^2 = .01$, $p < .05$). Similarly, when the 12-item SHRQ was used in place of the 21-item measure, an interaction effect was found for symptomatology ($\Delta R^2 = .01$, $p < .01$) and a marginally significant interaction with vigor ($\Delta R^2 = .01$, $p < .10$). Using the procedures suggested by Cohen, Cohen, West, and Aiken (2003, p. 269), both significant and marginally significant (exploratory) interaction effects were plotted (see Figures 2a through 2d; predicted scores) As Figures 2a through 2d suggest, individuals who self-described as using humor in a wide range of situations and who also experienced high levels of stress, reported higher levels of vigor and less symptomatology than those who used less humor.[25]

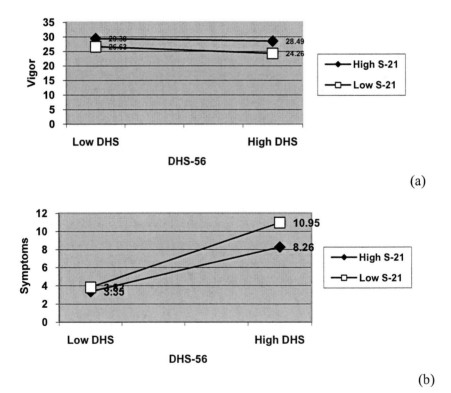

(a)

(b)

---

[25] 1 standard deviation above and below the mean.

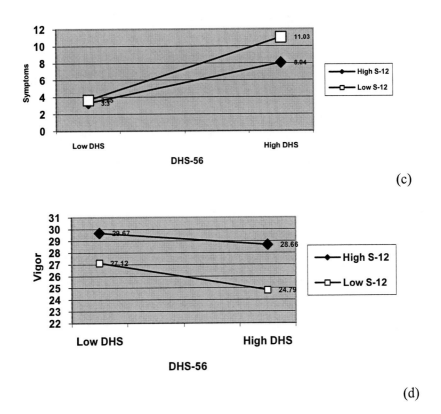

(c)

(d)

Figures 2. Interaction effects between the SHRQ-12 and SHRQ-21 and stress (DHS-56) in relation to vigor and symptomatology.
(a): SHRQ-21 by DHS-56: Vigor as the criterion ($p < .05$)
(b): SHRQ-21 by DHS-56: Symptoms as the criterion ($p < .05$)
(c): SHRQ-12 by DHS-56: Symptoms as the criterion ($p < .05$)
(d): SHRQ-12 by DHS-56: Vigor as the criterion ($p < .10$)

Direct effects were also found for both versions of the SHRQ in relation to both positive and negative mood. When positive mood was the criterion, both the 12-item SHRQ ($\beta = .28$, $p < .001$ and the 21-item SHRQ ($\beta = .32$, $p < .001$) were statistically significant. And last, the 12-item SHRQ ($\beta = -.19$, $p < .001$) and the 21-item SHRQ ($\beta = -.21$, $p < .001$) were each significant in predicting negative mood.

The Inventory of College Students Recent Life Experiences -17

Interestingly, when the Inventory of College Students Recent Life Experiences was the stress predictor, there was a marginally significant interaction with the full SHRQ measure in relation to positive mood ($\Delta R^2 =$ .01, $p < .10$). However, when the brief SHRQ was used, the interaction was significant ($\Delta R^2 = .01$, $p < .05$). Similarly, a marginally significant interaction was found between the 12-item SHRQ and the Inventory of College Students Recent Life Experiences in relation to symptomatology ($\Delta R^2 = .004$, $p < .10$). No significant or marginally significant interactions were found with respect to the 21-item version. To determine if these interactions paralleled the trends in Figures 1a through 1d, the three significant and marginally significant product-term interactions (i.e., predicted scores) were plotted. As Figures 3a through 3c suggest, under high stress, individuals who consistently reported using humor in a variety of situations, also tended to report experiencing more positive mood and less symptomatology relative to those who had low scores on the humor measures. For both the 12- and 21-item SHRQs, main effects were found in relation to vigor (12-item version: $\beta = .26$, $p < .001$; 21-item version: $\beta = .28$, $p < .001$) and negative mood (12-item version: $\beta = -.13$, $p < .001$; 21-item version: $\beta = -.13$, $p < .001$).

The Perceived Stress Scale

No significant interaction effects were found for either version of the SHRQ when the Perceived Stress Scale was the stress predictor, although at the third step of each analysis, both versions of the SHRQ predicted the criteria, with the exception of the symptomatology scale. Specifically, the SHRQ predicted positive mood (12 items: $\beta = .18$, $p < .001$; 21 items: $\beta = .21$, $p < .001$), negative mood (12 items: $\beta = -.08$, $p < .05$; 21 items: $\beta = -.09$, $p < .05$), and vigor (12 items: $\beta = .20$, $p < .001$; 21 items: $\beta = .23$, $p < .001$).

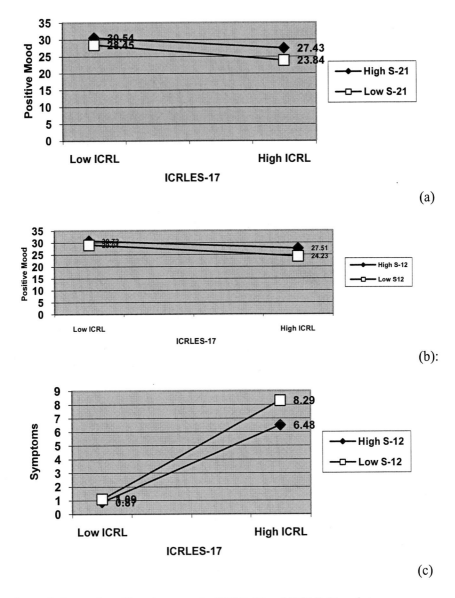

Figures 3. Interaction effects between the SHRQ-12 and SHRQ-21 and stress (ICRLES-17) in relation to positive mood and symptomatology.
(a): SHRQ-21 by ICRLES-17: Positive mood as the criterion ($p < .10$).
(b): SHRQ-12 by ICRLES-17: Positive mood as the criterion ($p < .05$).
(c): SHRQ-12 by ICRLES-17: Symptomatology as the criterion ($p < .10$).

DISCUSSION

The results from study 2 further suggests that the brief SHRQ may be a useful measure for researchers when time is limited or when mass testing is involved. Generally, the results from the second study indicate that the 12-item measure possesses an acceptable level of internal consistency (albeit with some variability between men and women and between the 12- and 21-item versions) and corresponds quite highly with the 21-item measure. Further, no sex differences were found for either scale and the same personality and mood variables were found to predict both the 12- and 21-item measures. The 12-item measure was also found to moderate 2 of the 3 stress variables on health.

Study 3 expands on these findings by examining a broader range of personality, coping, stress, health status, and demographic variables in relation to both SHRQs.

Chapter 4

STUDY 3

METHOD

PARTICIPANTS AND PROCEDURE

Questionnaire data were collected from 115 university students ($n_{men} = 20$, $n_{women} = 95$). The mean age was found to be 18.87 (SD = 1.83). Each of the questionnaires was administered in a small group setting. Informed consent was obtained. With the exception of the SHRQ-21, the Inventory of College Students Recent Life Experiences (49-item version; see study 2), and MacMillan's Health Opinion Survey (symptoms/illness behavior; study 2), the remaining measures were distinct from those administered in studies 1 and 2.[26]

Measures

1) *The Humor Styles Questionnaire* (HSQ; Martin et al., 2003). The HSQ is a 32-item questionnaire designed to assess four distinct

---

[26] The full ICSRLE is comprised of the following subscales: Developmental Challenge, Time Pressures, Academic Alienation, Romantic Problems, Assorted Annoyances, General Social, Mistreatment, and Friendship Problems.

humour styles; *Self-Enhancing* (e.g., "If I am feeling depressed, I can usually cheer myself up with humor"), *Affiliative* (e.g., "I enjoy making people laugh"), *Aggressive* (e.g., "If I don't like someone, I often use humor or teasing to put them down"), and *Self-Defeating* (e.g., "I will often get carried away in putting myself down if it makes my family or friends laugh"). Each item is rated on a seven-point scale ranging from 1 = *Totally disagree* to 7 = *Totally agree*. High scores on each of the measures reflect greater levels of that construct. The HSQ has been found to be both valid and reliable.

2) *The International Item Pool (IPIP) NEO-Five Factor Model Short-Form Measure* (IPIP-FFM; John A. Johnson, personal communication, January 22, 2010). The IPIP-FFM is a 120-item measure (24 items per domain) designed to assess the five domains of Openness to Experience (e.g., "Have a vivid imagination"), Conscientiousness (e.g., "Carry out my plans"), Extraversion (e.g., "Make friends easily"), Agreeableness (e.g., "Trust others"), and Neuroticism (e.g., "Worry about things"), based somewhat on Costa and McCrae's five-factor NEO-PI-R™ model (Costa & McCrae, 1992). In addition to the five factors (domains), six facet scores (four items per facet) per domain can be calculated (i.e., five factors or domains + 30 facets). For Openness to Experience, these facets include imagination, artistic interests, emotionality, adventurousness, intellect, and liberalism. For Conscientiousness, the facets are self-efficacy, orderliness, dutifulness, achievement striving, self-discipline, and cautiousness. The general extraversion domain is subsumed by the following facets: friendliness, gregariousness, assertiveness, activity level, excitement seeking, and cheerfulness. Agreeableness is measured by the facets of trust, morality, altruism, cooperation, modesty, and sympathy. Last, the facets pertaining to Neuroticism include anxiety, anger, depression, self-consciousness, immoderation, and vulnerability. Each item is rated on a five-point scale ranging from 1 = *Very innacurate* to 5 = *Very accurate*. High scores on each of the

domain and facet variables reflect greater levels of that construct. The IPIP version of Costa and McCrae's model has been found to have acceptable levels of internal consistency and validity.

3) *The Brief COPE* (trait version; Carver, 1997). The Brief COPE trait version, is a 28-item measure designed to assess a wide range of coping styles (two items per measure) including self-distraction, active coping, denial, substance use, use of emotional support, use of instrumental support, behavioral disengagement, venting, positive reframing, planning, humor, acceptance, religion, and self-blame. Based on previous research conducted by the first author, nine additional, exploratory items were added to the end of the questionnaire and pertained to the use of music (five items; e.g., "I listen to music") and one's use of nature (e.g., "I spend some time in nature"). Each item is rated on a four-point scale ranging from 1 = *I usually don't do this at all* to 4 = *I usually do this a lot*. High scores on each of the scales indicate greater use of the respective coping style. The Brief COPE has been found to be relatively consistent with the full COPE measure (Carver, 1997).

4) *The Happiness Questionnaire* (SHQ; Lyubomirsky & Lepper, 1999). The SHQ is a four-item questionnaire designed to assess current levels of happiness. An example item is, "Compared to most of my peers, I consider myself:" scale follows. Each item is rated on one of three different rating scales (e.g., *Not a very happy person* to *A very happy person*, *Less happy* to *More happy*, and *Not at all* to *A great deal*). The SHQ has been found to be both valid and reliable as a measure of happiness. High scores indicate greater levels of happiness.

5) *Life Satisfaction* (SWLS; Diener, Emmons, Larson, & Griffin, 1985). The SWLS is a reliable and valid five-item measure of general life satisfaction. Each of the positively phrased items (e.g., "If I could live my life over, I would change almost nothing") is rated on a seven-point scale from 1 = *Strongly disagree* to 7 = *Strongly agree*. High scores reflect greater levels of life satisfaction.

6) *Scale of Positive and Negative Experience* (SPANE; Diener et al., 2009). The 12-item SPANE was used to measure both positive (e.g., pleasant; six items) and negative (e.g., afraid) affect. Based on the past two weeks, participants are requested to rate each item on a five-point scale ranging from 1 = *Very Rarely or Never* to 5 = *Very Often or Always*. Higher self-reported scores on both measures indicates greater levels of positive and negative affect, respectively. The SPANE has been found to be both valid and reliable.

7) *Demographic and Health Questionnaire* (Korotkov, 2010). A detailed demographic questionnaire was used in the present study. The following questions and constructs were assessed: sex of participant, age, student status (full- or part-time), current year of study, courses currently taking, completed university courses, mother and fathers' achieved levels of education, family health conditions/background, two measures of expected longevity, general health status, employment status, number of siblings, five questions pertaining to religion and spirituality, and one question concerned with religious affiliation.

RESULTS

Overview

Descriptive statistics were first calculated for each of the measures. As in the previous two studies, the brief and full version of the SHRQ were found to be highly correlated. Further correlational analyses indicated that the SHRQs were related to several five-factor, coping, and health related variables. Principal components analyses once again supported the construct validity of both humor measures. Regression analyses indicated that several variables including extraversion, positive reframing, happiness, positive affect, general health, and religious/spiritual practices, predicted both SHRQs. Few sex differences were found; of those statistically significant, chance appears to have played a role. Overall, the results from Study 3 suggest that the 12-item SHRQ measure was related to a wider range of humor and nonhumor related constructs.

Descriptive Statistics

The means, standard deviations, and correlations (in relation to both SHRQs) for each of the variables can be found in Charts 4 through 7. Coefficient alpha for the full SHRQ was found to be .77 (males = .70; females = .79), and .65 for the 12-item version (males = .50[27]; females = .69), albeit smaller than those coefficients found in the first two studies. The 12- and 21-item measures were highly correlated ($r = .93$).

Examination of the correlations across each of the Charts reveals several interesting observations. For example, relatively few differences were found between the relationships of each SHRQ with personality (five-factor model), coping, health, stress, and demographic variables; in several instances, the correlations were larger for the shorter SHRQ version. Further, both SHRQs were correlated more strongly with the extraversion and agreeableness scales and less so with the other five-factor measures (Chart 4). The SHRQs were also correlated with both self-enhancing and affiliative humor styles, as well as several trait coping styles including emotional support, instrumental support, positive reframing, humor, and religion (Chart 5).

Further, when correlations were run for our health and SHRQ measures (Chart 6), both humor variables were found to be positively related to positive affect, happiness, and general health. There was also a marginally significant negative correlation between both humor measures and negative affect (see study 2 correlation matrix; in Study 2, the humor to negative affect correlation was significant). Generally, individuals who

---

[27] Keep in mind our n of 20 for the men of the sample. As the results from Study 3 further indicate, despite the small alpha, both SHRQs performed relatively similar.

rated themselves as more likely to laugh across a range of situations were also more likely to experience positive affect, happiness, and better health.

Chart 4. Correlations, means, and standard deviations for the five-factor domains, facets and the SHRQ-12 and SHRQ-21

Five-Factor Model	Mean	SD	SHRQ-12	SHRQ-21
Openness to Experience				
Imagination	80.96	11.58	.11	.15
Artistic Interests	15.30	3.09	.09	.16
Emotionality	14.02	3.58	.03	.09
Adventurousness	15.77	2.89	.04	.08
Intellect	12.04	2.91	.18†	.16
Liberalism	12.57	3.86	.07	.07
	11.25	2.85	-.02	-.02
Conscientiousness	82.97	12.43	-.17†	-.18*
Self-Efficacy	15.06	2.41	-.034	-.04
Orderliness	12.94	4.45	-.10	-.09
Dutifulness	16.09	2.07	-.16†	-.21*
Achievement Striving	14.56	3.16	-.02	-.03
Self-Discipline	12.98	2.91	-.06	-.05
Cautiousness	11.34	3.89	-.26**	-.30***
Extraversion	84.90	13.17	.44***	.43***
Friendliness	15.14	3.41	.35***	.34***
Gregariousness	14.08	4.00	.36***	.37***
Assertiveness	13.14	3.78	.27**	.25**
Activity Level	12.94	2.81	.03	.06
Excitement-Seeking	13.90	3.40	.31***	.33***
Cheerfulness	15.70	2.86	.33***	.29**
Agreeableness	92.53	8.94	.07	.09
Trust	13.06	3.67	.09	.12
Morality	16.57	2.63	-.19*	-.19*
Altruism	16.70	2.37	.15	.19*
Cooperation	15.70	2.88	-.00	-.02
Modesty	14.23	3.00	-.06	-.04
Sympathy	16.26	2.58	.23*	.23*
Neuroticism	71.28	14.76	.16†	-.12
Anxiety	14.10	3.79	-.18*	-.09
Anger	11.71	3.78	-.06	-.07
Depression	9.41	3.74	-.14	-.14
Self-Consciousness	11.68	3.86	-.27**	-.26**
Immoderation	12.08	3.08	.13	.13
Vulnerability	12.30	3.25	-.05	.01

*$p < .05$, **$p < .01$, ***$p < .001$, †$p < .10$.

Chart 5. Correlations, means, and standard deviations for the Brief COPE scales and the SHRQ-12 and SHRQ-21

Humor Styles/Brief COPE	Mean	SD	SHRQ-12	SHRQ-21
Self-enhancing Humor	37.97	7.21	.48***	.45***
Self-defeating Humor	28.78	8.37	.03	.03
Aggressive Humor	29.29	7.57	.15	.10
Affiliative Humor	46.97	6.78	.30**	.27**
Self-distraction	5.83	1.44	.09	.04
Active coping	5.69	1.24	-.00	-.03
Denial	3.22	1.57	.07	.15
Substance use	3.40	1.67	.00	.02
Use of emotional support	5.51	1.73	.18†	.21*
Use of instrumental support	5.78	1.71	.21*	.17†
Behavioral disengagement	3.57	1.38	.08	.08
Venting	4.97	1.47	.12	.13
Positive reframing	5.33	1.71	.27**	.25**
Planning	5.53	1.35	-.07	-.06
Humor	4.42	1.68	.37***	.34***
Acceptance	5.84	1.46	-.00	-.01
Religion	3.62	2.00	.27**	.25**
Self-blame	5.16	1.68	.08	.11
Music	13.07	4.31	.09	.06
Nature	9.01	3.76	.15	.09

$*p < .05$, $**p < .01$, $***p < .001$, $†p < .10$.

Chart 6. Correlations, means, and standard deviations for the stress and health variables and the SHRQ-12 and SHRQ-21

Stress/Health Scale	Mean	SD	SHRQ-12	SHRQ-21
ICSRLE Total	106.03	18.62	-.12	-.12
Developmental Challenge	24.83	5.71	-.13	-.13
Time Pressures	18.43	4.04	-.10	-.12
Academic Alienation	6.60	2.39	.01	-.00
Romantic Problems	6.53	2.62	-.03.	-.00
Assorted Annoyances	8.90	2.63	.08	.02
Gen. Social Mistreatment	11.84	3.72	-.16†	-.14
Friendship Problems	6.29	2.31	-.10	-.11
Happiness	19.92	4.85	.29**	.26**
Life Satisfaction	23.06	6.39	.10	.10
Perceived Symptomatology	24.63	6.91	-.09	-.10
Positive Affect	22.79	3.09	.21*	.22*
Negative Affect	15.88	4.46	-.17†	-.17†
General Health	3.40	.94	21*	.21*
Expected Life Span	.00	1.86	.14	.11
Family Health Background	9.41	4.98	-.06	.01

Note: Two items on the questionnaire measured expected life expectancy, an open-ended question as well as a categorical item. Both items were highly correlated with each other with a coefficient of .73. As such, each item was standardized and summed to form a composite measure. $^*p < .05$, $^{**}p < .01$, $^{***}p < .001$, $^\dagger p < .10$.

The SHRQs were also correlated with a small number of demographic variables. As Chart 7 indicates, both measures were related to number of siblings (marginally with the 12-item SHRQ), religious practices, and religious affiation. The 21-item measure was marginally correlated with number of courses completed. Interpreted, those self-reporting with higher SHRQ scores also reported having more siblings, engaging in more religious/spiritual practices, and self-described as being religious. For the marginal correlation, humor was loosely related to fewer courses completed.

Chart 7. Correlations, means, and standard deviations for the demographic variables and the SHRQ-12 and SHRQ-21

Demographic Variable	Mean	SD	SHRQ-12	SHRQ-21
Sex	-	-	-.03	-.03
Age	18.87	1.83	-.07	-.13
Student Status (full, part)	-	-	.08	-.02
Year at university	1.52	.74	-.05	-.08
Number courses current	4.77	.78	-.04	-.07
Number courses completed	4.43	7.02	-.14	-.17†
Mother's Education$^\Delta$	6.00	2.00	.08	.15
Father's Education$^\Delta$	4.00	2.18	.04	.00
Number of Siblings	4.23	1.39	-.15†	-.19*
Religion/Spirituality	.00	4.20	.22*	.22*
Religious Affiliation*	1.66	.48	.25**	.24*

Note: *Religious affiliation coded 2 for religious and 1 for not religious (Atheist and Agnostic; Agnostic coded as not religious given its low frequency). Seventy-six participants fell into the religious category and 39 into the not religious category. The two-category variable correlated .52 ($p < .001$) with the religion question while a three category variable (religious, agnostic, atheist) correlated .47 ($p < .001$) with the religion question. $^*p < .05$, $^{**}p < .01$, $^{***}p < .001$, $^\dagger p < .10$.

$^\Delta$ Mode is reported here (4 = Completed community college; 4 = Completed secondary school).

Overall, humorous SHRQ individuals tended toward being somewhat extraverted and agreeable. They also tended to adopt more self-enhancing and affiliative humor styles, and to make use of their supports (emotional, instrumental) to cope, to cognitively reframe their stressful encounters, to use humor to cope, and to engage in various religious practices. Although both SHRQs were uncorrelated with various stress measures as assessed by the Inventory of College Students Recent Life Experiences, unlike Study 2 in which the sample size was larger, they were related somewhat to health, in particular, greater levels of happiness, positive affect, and general health.

Chart 8. Principal components analysis (promax rotation) pattern matrix: The SHRQ (21 items), five-factor model, humor styles, stress, and health

Variable	Components				
	1	2	3	4	5
Negative Affect	**-.866**	.042	.050	.078	-.029
Happiness	**.820**	.220	-.102	-.127	.123
Positive Affect	**.806**	.198	-.269	.268	.070
Life Satisfaction	**.749**	.040	-.068	.189	.169
Neuroticism	**-.625**	-.039	-.163	.271	-.247
ICSRLE(49)	**-.528**	.141	**-.435**	-.163	.235
Extraversion	.181	**.730**	.160	-.106	.309
SHRQ(21)	.050	**.688**	.147	.119	-.193
Affiliative Humor	-.050	**.667**	.290	-.064	-.073
Self-Enhancing Humor	**.490**	**.569**	-.033	.141	-.198
Expected Life Span	-.334	.372	**.892**	.182	.004
General Health	-.064	.311	**.733**	-.092	.155
Physical Symptoms	**-.455**	.108	**-.459**	.185	.290
Agreeableness	.183	-.009	.092	**.818**	-.119
Aggressive Humor	.057	.381	-.063	**-.689**	-.199
Openness to Experience	-.109	.376	.011	**.651**	-.013
Self-Defeating Humor	-.189	.102	-.005	.039	**-.777**
Conscientiousness	.176	-.266	**.482**	.173	**.492**

Construct Validity

To assess the construct validity of the 12- and 21-item SHRQs, we ran a series of principal components analyses (promax rotation). Given the large number of variables, we ran separate analyses for the two SHRQs in relation to the coping variables, the five-factor model domain markers, stress, the health variables, as well as the humor style markers.

The SHRQ and the Five-Factor Model, Humor Styles, Stress, and Health

The first set of analyses examined both SHRQs in relation to the five factors of openness to experience, conscientiousness, extraversion, agreeableness, and neuroticism, as well as the four humor styles (affiliative, self-enhancing, aggressive, and self-defeating), stress (total

ICSRLE), and the health (affect, symptomatology, general health, satisfaction, happiness) constructs. The component solution can be found in Chart 8. The first analysis used the 21-item SHRQ. As Chart 8 suggests, the 21-item SHRQ loaded most highly on component 2 (out of five components), along with the extraversion domain marker, and the two positive based humor styles, affiliative humor and self-enhancing humor. This component seems to reflect a 'Social Extraversion' or a 'Positive based Personality' variable. This solution accounted for 65.57 % of the variance in the measures.

Chart 9. Principal components analysis (promax rotation) pattern matrix: The SHRQ (12 items), five-factor model, humor styles, stress, and health

Variable	Components				
	1	2	3	4	5
Negative Affect	**-.859**	.048	.035	.085	-.030
Positive Affect	**.815**	.175	-.266	.277	.065
Happiness	**.815**	.223	-.095	-.122	.120
Life Satisfaction	**.752**	.026	-.061	.190	.164
Neuroticism	**-.613**	-.052	-.173	.277	-.249
ICSRLE (49)	**-.515**	.145	-.456	-.150	.233
Extraversion	.189	**.722**	.140	-.085	.313
SHRQ (12)	.035	**.710**	.162	.077	-.174
Affiliative Humor	-.045	**.673**	.273	-.033	-.081
Self-Enhancing Humor	.494	**.563**	-.035	.164	-.204
Expected Life Span Composite	-.340	.384	**.885**	.194	.000
General Health	-.072	.316	**.727**	-.093	.164
Conscientiousness	.167	-.256	**.493**	.157	**.488**
Physical Symptoms	**-.441**	.109	**-.473**	.197	.281
Agreeableness	.190	-.030	.102	**.819**	-.127
Openness	-.087	.343	-.004	**.669**	-.018
Aggressive Humor	.055	**.400**	-.076	**-.667**	-.200
Self-Defeating Humor	-.189	.103	-.003	.054	**-.781**

Chart 10. Principal components analysis (promax rotation) pattern matrix: The SHRQ (21 items) and coping trait variables

Variable	Components						
	1	2	3	4	5	6	7
Self-Blame Coping	**.787**	.083	-.024	-.109	.143	.202	.017
Denial Coping	**.748**	.003	-.032	.223	-.199	-.195	-.111
Behavioral Disengagement Coping	**.736**	-.150	-.077	.030	-.163	-.115	-.087
Venting Coping	**.501**	.303	.276	-.011	.007	.033	.394
Planning Coping	.097	**.906**	-.073	-.074	-.060	.087	-.014
Active Coping	-.082	**.824**	-.030	-.052	.122	-.111	-.121
Emotional Support Coping	.054	-.088	**.944**	-.039	-.025	-.053	-.114
Instrumental Support Coping	-.165	-.039	**.885**	.052	.018	.124	.020
Humour Coping	.117	.020	-.152	**.885**	-.033	.143	.176
SHRQ (21)	.011	-.184	.169	**.727**	-.095	-.018	.029
PositiveReframing Coping	-.150	**.433**	-.018	**.489**	.094	.119	-.237
Nature Coping	-.138	.031	-.032	-.117	**.922**	.011	.099
Religion Coping	-.008	.104	.109	.315	**.520**	-.323	.038
Acceptance Coping	-.185	.055	.058	.148	-.279	**.795**	.031
Self-Distraction Coping	.155	-.061	.005	-.030	.335	**.637**	-.093
Substance Use Coping	-.036	-.323	-.102	.188	.216	.040	**.856**
Music Coping	.247	-.241	.018	.061	.213	.156	**-.610**

We next repeated the same analyses (Chart 9) with the 12-item SHRQ to determine if it would load on a similar component and with the same variables. Once again, PCA (promax rotation) yielded a similar component structure, loading with extraversion, and the two positive humor styles, affiliative and self-enhancing humor. Unlike the previous analysis, the aggressive humor style also loaded marginally on this component. In the first analysis with the 21-item SHRQ, the loading was found to be .38, close but just below our .40 loading cut-off. In any case, it is interesting that aggressive humor had the smallest loading onto this component (and was positive), suggesting that it does not have a strong weighting in the interpretation of this component. This solution accounted for 65.69 % of the variance in the measures.

Trait Coping

The second set of analyses examined both SHRQs in relation to the 16 trait coping resources (Chart 10). Examination of the output indicated that 69.53 % of the variance was accounted for in this seven-component solution. When the full SHRQ was used, it loaded most strongly on the 4th component, which was comprised of two other variables above the .40 loading cut-off, the humor scale (COPE), and the positive reframing scale.

When the 12-item SHRQ was used in a follow-up analysis, it also loaded on the fourth component, along with the humor scale (Brief COPE), positive reframing, and positive reframing (69.53 % of the variance was accounted for by this solution; Chart 11); although religion as a coping resource loaded the highest onto this component (.35), relative to the other components, it was below our .40 loading cut-off. Interestingly, the analyses yielded a six-component solution, unlike the seven-component solution when the 21-item measure was used. It appears that in the seven-component solution with the 21-item SHRQ, the substance and music coping variables broke off into a separate component. Despite this, the 12-item SHRQ solution yielded a similar pattern of findings with the SHRQ loading with the same variables (humor, positive reframing) as in the 21-item SHRQ solution. Given the variables loading on this component, it seems to best reflect a "Coping Humor" variable.

Thus, overall, the 12-item SHRQ performed in a similar manner to that of the 21-item version, once again suggesting that the former possesses comparable levels of construct validity.

SHRQ Correlates

We next examined the various personality, coping, stress, humor, and health related correlates of both SHRQs with the expectation that the 12-item version would be predicted by the same variables as the parent measure. Given our small sample size we decided to run separate stepwise multiple regression analyses for the five-factor model facets, coping, humor style, as well as the stress, health, and demographic variables (predictors). In each case, only the variables that were statistically correlated at the .05 level were used in the analyses (see Charts 4 through 7).

Humor Styles

For the first analysis, the 21-item measure was regressed on both affiliative and self-enhancing humor style scores. The results indicated that the self-enhancing humor style was the lone predictor ($\beta = .45$, $p < .001$; $R^2 = .20$). Similarly, the 12-item SHRQ was regressed on the same two styles. In this analysis, as in the previous one, the self-enhancing humor style was the only variable of the two to predict the criterion ($\beta = .46$, $p < .001$; $R^2 = .23$).

Chart 11. Principal components analysis (promax rotation) pattern matrix: The SHRQ (12 items), five-factor model, humor styles, stress, and health

Variable	Components					
	1	2	3	4	5	6
Self-Blame Coping	**.814**	.076	.016	-.129	.216	.162
Denial Coping	**.695**	-.005	-.127	.162	-.009	-.236
Behavioral Disengagement Coping	**.666**	-.198	-.148	.034	.021	-.145
Venting Coping	**.557**	.280	.368	.004	-.291	.044
Planning Coping	.108	**.908**	-.079	-.095	-.106	.102
Active Coping	-.070	**.836**	-.019	-.043	.061	-.104
Emotional Support Coping	.006	-.100	**.896**	-.067	.084	-.085
Instrumental Support Coping	-.178	-.048	**.879**	.061	.001	.107
Humor Coping	.142	.034	-.161	**.906**	-.152	.129
SHRQ(12)	-.091	-.231	.147	**.732**	.012	.017
Positive Reframing Coping	-.168	**.455**	-.069	**.485**	.213	.097
Religion Coping	.075	.150	.230	.348	.274	-.347
Music Coping	.169	-.235	-.090	.060	**.727**	.074
Nature Coping	.032	.094	.228	-.038	**.581**	-.013
Substance Use Coping	.169	-.276	.148	.215	**-.499**	.081
Acceptance Coping	-.198	.050	-.008	.116	-.106	**.800**
Self-Distraction Coping	.203	-.049	.063	-.001	**.461**	**.596**

Five-Factor Model

In the first set of analyses, the 21-item SHRQ was regressed on dutifulness, cautiousness, friendliness, gregariousness, assertiveness, excitement seeking, cheerfulness, morality, altruism, sympathy, and self-consciousness measures. In this analysis, gregariousness ($\beta = .27$, $p < .01$), cautiousness ($\beta = -.22$, $p < .05$), and assertiveness ($\beta = .20$, $p < .05$) predicted the criterion ($R^2 = .21$). The second analysis regressed the 12-item measure on cautiousness, friendliness, gregariousness, assertiveness, excitement seeking, cheerfulness, morality, sympathy, anxiety, as well as self-consciousness. As in the first analysis with the 21-item SHRQ, gregariousness ($\beta = 27$, $p < .005$), assertiveness ($\beta = .22$, $p < .01$), and cautiousness ($\beta = -.18$, $p < .05$) were all significant ($R^2 = .21$). Interpreted, those who self-rated as being gregarious, assertive, and less cautious, were also more likely to laugh and smile more frequently.

Trait Coping Styles (Brief COPE)

We next regressed the 21-item SHRQ on both self-enhancing and affiliative humor styles, as well as emotional support, positive reframing, humor, and religion. Two variables predicted this criterion, coping humor ($\beta = .33$, $p < .001$) and emotional support ($\beta = .18$, $p < .05$; $R^2 = .15$). Similar though not equivalent findings were obtained when we substituted the longer humor measure with the 12-item version. The same predictors were used to predict the criterion, save emotional support, and with the addition of the instrumental support coping variable. The output from this analysis indicated that humor ($\beta = .35$, $p < .001$) and instrumental support ($\beta = .17$, $p < .05$), predicted scores on the 12-item SHRQ ($R^2 = .17$).

Health

We last examined which health variables predicted both SHRQ outcomes. In the first analysis, the 21-item SHRQ was regressed on happiness, positive affect, and the one-item general health measure. The results from this analysis indicated that happiness ($\beta = .26$, $p < .01$) was the sole predictor ($R^2 = .07$). A similar result was found when we regressed the

12-item SHRQ on the same three variables. In this case, happiness (β = .29, p < .01) scores predicted scores on the humor questionnaire (R^2 = .09).

Demographics

The 21-item SHRQ was regressed on the two religion variables (i.e., religion/spirituality, religious affiliation) as well as number of siblings. The analyses revealed that both religious affiliation (β = .23, p < .05) and number of siblings (β = -.19, p < .05) predicted the criterion (R^2 = .09). Thus, individuals who scored high on the SHRQ also reported having more siblings and being religious. When we regressed the 12-item SHRQ on the two religion questions, religious affiliation (β = .25, p < .01) predicted the humor criterion (R^2 = .06).

Sex Differences

As in Study 1 and Study 2, we assessed for the main effects of sex, humor (12- and 21-item SHRQs), as well as their interactions; the five factors (domains, facets), coping, stress (ICSRLE, subscales), health, and demographic variables served as the outcome variables. Exactly 81 tests for each SHRQ were conducted. Overall, for both SHRQs, few significant sex differences (interactions) were found for most of the variables.[28] For the emotionality construct (Openness to Experience), there was a marginally significant sex by SHRQ interaction (p < .10) for the 12-item measure and a significant interaction (p < .05) for the 21-item version. Generally, the men of the sample who scored high on the SHRQ were also found to self-report with higher scores on the emotionality construct. For the immoderation construct (Neuroticism), a significant interaction (p < .05) was found for the 12-item measure but not the full measure. When the 12-item SHRQ was used, the men who reported that they would smile and laugh in a variety of situations also reported being more immoderate relative to the women. Because of the number of tests and the failure to

---

[28] Given the number of tests (162) and the number of significant interactions (4), the latter may be attributed to chance factors.

replicate this specific finding when the 21-item SHRQ was used, this result is suspect. There was also a significant interaction in relation to the self-defeating humor style construct for both SHRQs (both $p < .05$). The men of the sample who laughed and smiled the most, reported a corresponding decrease in the use of this humor style unlike the women who reported more self-defeating humor. A marginally significant interaction ($p < .10$) was found for the 12-item SHRQ in relation to the expected life span construct and a significant interaction for the parent SHRQ measure ($p < .05$). When we plotted this latter interaction, the males of the sample with high scores on the SHRQ measure, reported a lower expected life expectancy relative to the females who reported a greater expectancy. No other interactions were found. Sex was also not correlated with either SHRQ measure (see Chart 7).

Overall, there were few sex differences differences found; in some cases, the effect was not replicated across both SHRQs. These findings support the results found in Study 1 and Study 2 that the brief SHRQ performed in a similar manner to that of the 21-item version. However, caution is warrented in that for both Study 1 and Study 3, there were fewer males in the sample relative to females. In any case, because the measures performed similarly, the findings are encouraging.

DISCUSSION

Overall, the findings from Study 3 provide further support for the brief SHRQ we report herein. Both measures were found to be correlated at similar magnitudes with the same variables, with only a few exceptions. The SHRQs were correlated with a range of personality (e.g., extraversion), coping (e.g., reappraisal, support), health (e.g., happiness, positive affect), and demographic variables. A series of PCAs replicated the SHRQ structures and the two measures, with only a handful of exceptions, were predicted by a range of personality, coping, health, and demographic variables. And last, there was little significant evidence for any sex differences; both SHRQs performed in a similar manner when compared to the variables studied herein. No sex differences were also found for either SHRQ.

Chapter 5

CONCLUSIONS

A bossy sort of fellow strides into a lunchroom and says to the
maître d' in a loud voice, "Is this really a first class restaurant?"
"Indeed it is, sir," the captain says. "But that's all right –
you can come in anyway."

- Steve Allen (in Allen & Wollman, 1998)

We set out to develop a brief measure of the SHRQ, a widely used measure of the sense of humor construct. The data from our three studies suggests that the 12-item version of the SHRQ appears to be both reliable and valid as a brief version of its parent scale. The results also suggest that the brief SHRQ is able to detect a variety of health related benefits. Specifically, the 12-item SHRQ was found to (1) possess acceptable levels of internal consistency, (2) be for the most part, void of any sex differences, (3) be correlated with and predicted by a range of other humor and nonhumor scales (e.g., personality, coping), (4) be reasonably unrelated to a host of nonhumor variables, (5) moderate the relationship of stress on health, and (6) be predicted by various health and demographic measures.

Chart 12. Significant correlations between both SHRQs and personality, stress, health, coping, and demographic variables across all three studies

12-item	SHRQ 21-item SHRQ
Study 1	
• Funniness ratings (+), Humor Initiation and Response Measure (+), Sense of Humor Questionnaire (+), Coping Humor Scale (+)	• Funniness ratings (+), Humor Initiation and Response Measure (+), Sense of Humor Questionnaire (+), Coping Humor Scale (+)
Study 2	
• Happiness (+), extraversion (+), optimism (+), Stress (-), Perceived Stress Scale (-), physical symptoms (-), positive (+) , negative mood (-), and vigor (+)	• Happiness (+), extraversion (+), optimism (+), Stress (-), Perceived Stress Scale (-), physical symptoms (-), positive (+) , negative mood (-), and vigor (+)
Study 3	
• Cautiousness (-), extraversion (+), friendliness (+), gregariousness (+), assertiveness (+), excitement-seeking (+), cheerfulness (+), morality (-), sympathy (+), anxiety (-), self-consciousness (-)	• Conscientiousness (-), dutifulness (-), cautiousness (-), extraversion (+), friendliness (+), gregariousness (+), assertiveness (+), excitement-seeking (+), cheerfulness (+), morality (-), altruism (+), sympathy (+), anxiety (-), self-consciousness (-)
• Self-enhancing humor style (+), affiliative humor style (+)	• Self-enhancing humor style (+), affiliative humor style (+)
• Instrumental support coping (+), positive reframing coping (+), humor coping (+), religion coping (+)	• Emotional support coping (+), positive reframing coping (+), humor coping (+), religion coping (+)
• Happiness (+), positive affect (+), general health (+)	• Happiness (+), positive affect (+), general health (+)
• Religion/Spirituality practices (+), religious affiliation (+)	• Religion/Spirituality practices (+), religious affiliation (+)

Note. Only correlations significant at .05 level are reported.

PSYCHOMETRICS AND THE 12-ITEM SHRQ

The 12-item SHRQ was found to hold up well to our analyses. Although the internal consistency of the short version was found to be smaller in magnitude than the 21-item measure, the overall alphas, collapsed across sex, revealed relatively similar coefficients to those found in the literature, despite this variation. Further, in Study 1 both the Coping Humor Scale and the humor response item were found to predict the 12- and 21-item measures suggesting that individuals who report using humor as a coping strategy and who respond to situations with laughter, were also more likely to smile, laugh, and display or experience amusement across different situations. Study 2 extended these findings to other humor and nonhumor related measures. As in Study 1, the humor response item predicted scores on both SHRQs. In addition, optimism, extraversion, and vigor were also related to our two humor criteria. Individuals who self-described as optimistic, extraverted, and high in vigor, also reported using humor across a range of situations (SHRQ). In Study 3, extraversion (and its facets), two agreeableness facets, affiliative and self-enhancing humor, coping, health, and religious/spiritual practices, were related to both humor criteria.

The principal components analyses also bore similar solutions across the two humor measures. In all of the principal components analyses conducted, the SHRQs tended to load on the same components, and with the same variables in their respective analyses. For example, in Study 3, both SHRQs loaded on the same extraversion and coping components.

Overall, one interpretation of the data is that although the SHRQs are related to health outcome and the other constructs assessed herein, they are also somewhat independent of them. Thus, both the 12- and 21-item measures converged and diverged in expected ways with the other humor and nonhumor related constructs. To provide an overall view of these relationships, Chart 12 summarizes the variables that the SHRQs were correlated with across all three studies. As Chart 12 strongly suggests, there is a striking similarity in the performance of both SHRQs. Thus, despite the smaller alpha coefficients, relative to the 21-item version, the brief measure nonetheless performed well.

HUMOR, STRESS MODERATION, PERSONALITY, AND COPING

Generally, the findings provide support for both direct effect and moderator models. The results from Study 2 suggests that individuals who laughed and otherwise smiled across a range of situations and who experienced high levels of stress (DHS56, ICSRLE-17, save PSS), also tended to report less physical and behavioral symptomatology, as well as greater levels of vigor and positive mood, than those who self-described as less humorous. In addition, the pattern of the interactions was found to be similar across both measures. Generally, these findings support and extend previous studies linking the SHRQ to well-being and perceived physical health (e.g., Abel, 1998; Lefcourt & Martin, 1986; see also Kerkkänen, Kuiper, & Martin, 2004 for a different perspective). The analyses (Study 2) also revealed that both versions of the SHRQ were related (direct effects) to a variety of stress (PSS and the ICSRLE-17) and health related criteria including increased positive mood and vigor, as well as decreased negative mood and perceived physical symptomatology (see e.g., Martin, 1996, 2001, 2007). In Study 1 and Study 3, both SHRQs were unrelated to stress; in these cases, the relatively small sample sizes may have played a part. Overall, humor appears to be beneficial during high periods of stress and cross-situationally where stress is not an issue.

The SHRQs were also found to be related to personality, humor style, and coping. These findings support previous research linking the SHRQ to a broad body of psychosocial indicators (e.g., Martin et al., 2003). Not surprisingly, the SHRQs were linked to extraversion and its facets indicating that the latter may tend to laugh and smile more relative to introverts (see e.g., Ruch & Deckers, 1993). The SHRQs were also clearly related to self-enhancing and affiliative humor styles although the former best predicted scores on the SHRQs. Essentially, individuals who laugh also appear to use humor to self-enhance or to help cope with the difficulties of life; they also appear to be quite affiliative. Their scores on the extraversion measures appear to indirectly support this (see Martin et al., 2003). And last, the SHRQs were also related to a number of coping variables, in particular, support, positive reframing, and religion. As we discussed in the introduction, some research has linked humor to both support, as well as the appraisal process (e.g., Dixon, 1980). Not surprisingly, these data suggest that humor and laughter may be useful in dealing with stress by enabling individuals to distance themselves from the stressor or to view it in a different light. Humor may also be significant within both instrumental and emotional support contexts. One limitation here is that our coping measure was trait based. Although there is some support for a trait based model of coping, others (e.g., Lazarus & Folkman, 1984) have argued for a situationally based construction of the coping concept.[29]

IMPLICATIONS, LIMITATIONS, AND SUGGESTIONS FOR FURTHER RESEARCH

The data presented herein suggests that the brief SHRQ is a useful tool for researchers interested in examining the health enhancing effects of humor. In particular, the results suggest that the brief version may be useful in several distinct research contexts (e.g., mass testing, time sensitive conditions). Further, although the findings shed additional light on the SHRQ, and humor and laughter responsiveness in general, some caution is warranted concerning these findings. First, the usual caveats surrounding the use of correlational data should be noted. That is, although we have suggested that those who self-report as using humor across a range of situations are more likely to experience less stress and fewer

---

[29] As such, we were remiss to assess for mediation effects.

health problems, it is also possible that those who report feeling good about themselves (e.g., positive mood) may also be more likely to laugh and use humor. For example, some research (e.g., Deckers, 1998) suggests that positive mood may also enhance the effectiveness of some individuals'use of humor. Theoretically, the behavioral model may help to explain such conclusions. For example, in describing the role of reinforcement that we suggested earlier, we speculate that mood (distal) may modify the direct (proximal) antecedents (e.g., humorous cue) in prompting humor use.

A second limitation is that other third variables (e.g., neuroticism) not incorporated into these studies may help to explain the moderating (or confounding) effects of humor on health (see e.g., Korotkov & Hannah, 1994). For example, in Korotkov and Hannah, when neuroticism was controlled for, the moderating effects of coping humor were no longer significant. Thus, (controlled) prospective and experimental multivariate research designs would be helpful in clarifying these relationships.

Although this study found the SHRQ to moderate the effects of stress on health, further exploration concerning the theoretical processes or mechanisms linking humor to stress and health would be useful. In general, such mechanisms may focus on the biopsychosocial variables that help to transmit the effects of an independent or predictor variable (e.g., humor) to a dependent or criterion variable (e.g., health). More complex models are also possible (e.g., moderated mediation; see e.g., MacKinnon, 2008). However, in supporting Friedman (2000) and others (e.g., Korotkov, 2010a, 2010b; Roberts et al., 2007) who point out that empirical studies linking personality in general, to health, have failed to adequately test such intervening variables, Martin (2002) similarly indicates that despite widespread media reports concerning the benefits of humor, support for these processes remains tentative (see also e.g., Kuiper, Grimshaw, Leite, & Kirsh, 2004).

Further to this, the models discussed in the introduction section, reviews, extends, and reinforces the various potential mechanisms that may help to understand such processes. For example, humor use may, as suggested by those espousing the incongruity model, support a distancing function (e.g., escape or avoidance; e.g., O'Connell, 1976). The juxtaposition of two disparate ideas may influence such efforts. Alternatively, laughter or humor may allow for a significant reduction in physiological arousal (e.g., Berlyne, 1972). Superiority or disparagement theorists may further argue that humor use allows one to master a demanding situation in order to regain control and raise esteem levels (e.g., Levine, 1977; see also behavioral models re: social cognitive theory). And last, behaviorists would argue that humor use and laughter could serve multiple functions. For example, laughter may help to attract social attention as well as decrease sensory overload. Conversely, laughter may help to increase underload in those situations where, for example, boredom is significant. The stress moderating effects observed in our research requires follow-up in order to assess each of these possible functions as well as to examine the isomorphic nature of these functions with the other theories.

Just as it is important to elucidate the mechanisms linking humor to positive health, it is also valuable to determine and highlight those factors that prompt or promote (state) humor use in the first place.[30] Surprisingly, few studies have been conducted in this vein. For example, as alluded to earlier, some research suggests that being in a positive mood may have a significant impact on humor use (Deckers, 1998).[31] The literature also suggests that humor motivation and communication may be influential factors in the production of humor (Feingold & Mazella, 1993). Given these data, we suggest that a more complex and combined trait/affective, cognitive social learning, and biobehavioral model may be of some benefit in explaining humor use (e.g., efficacy, self-regulation) and improved health status. That is, we recommend that researchers move beyond or

---

[30] As should be evident, one limitation of trait based approaches to humor assessment is that traits tend to be static and relatively unchanging constructs. This contrasts with those paradigms (e.g., social-learning) and world views which suggest that humor can be learned (modeled and corrected) as well as self-regulated in various social contexts. Thus, humor could also be viewed as a changeable or changing construct, one reflecting impermanence as opposed to permanence.

[31] Some research also suggests that humor production can be increased through priming. For example, in Lehman et al. (2001), it was found that participants in a humor video (priming) instructional group produced more humorous narratives.

complement simple trait based approaches to humor use to focus additional energies on humor generation and its impact on stress and health. The model we present in Figure 4 reflects this perspective.

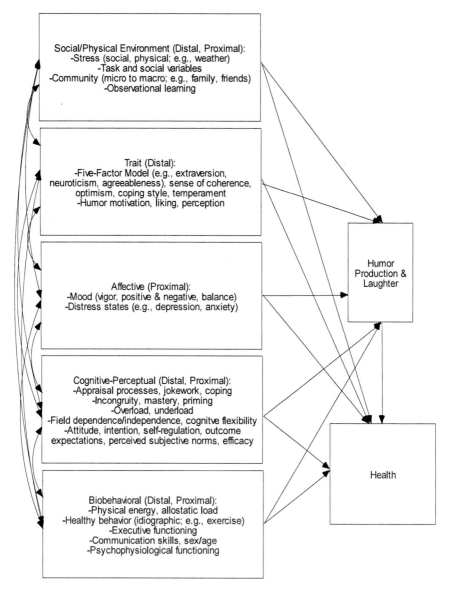

Figure 4. Humor and health model.

We further suggest that researchers consider both the distal and proximal antecedents (see e.g., Eysenck, 1997; see also Figure 4) to humor use, both idiographically and nomothetically, as well as dynamically (e.g., bidirectional paths), in order to incorporate such factors into their own models.[32] While admittedly not comprehensive and specific, the model we propose combines in particular, both trait and cognitive social learning approaches. At this point in our study, we make no assumptions concerning the precise mediating influences of humor production and subsequent health impacts, given in part the often dynamic interchanges that occur with such variables (e.g., positive mood as both an antecedent and consequence of humor). However, the model itself does move beyond simple antecedent-mediator-consequence models and suggests, as many have speculated on, other person-health based processes or pathways (e.g., extraversion and health; see e.g., Friedman, 2008 and Korotkov, 2010a, 2010b). Indeed, the web of causation we advance is ultimately, highly complex (see e.g., Figure 4, implied covariances).

SUMMARY AND CONCLUSIONS

The purpose of this text was to focus on the development of a brief version of the Situational Humor Response Questionnaire. In doing so, we briefly discussed the current state of the literature and suggested that researchers may benefit from a pared down version of the SHRQ. Using data from three studies, the results suggest that the brief SHRQ we described herein represents a reliable and valid measure for use in situations where mass testing takes place, where time may be an issue, and in other situations the researcher or clinician deems appropriate.

---

[32] Some of the unidirectional paths presented in Figure 3 are in actuality bidirectional. The use of one way arrows was meant to simplify the model.

REFERENCES

Abel, M.H. (1998). Interaction of humor and gender in moderating relationships between stress and outcomes. *The Journal of Psychology, 132*, 267 – 276.

Abel, M.H. (2002). Humor, stress, and coping strategies. *Humor: International Journal of Humor Research, 15*, 365 – 381.

Allen, S., & Wollman, J. (1998). *How to be funny: Discovering the comic in you*. Amherst, NY: Prometheus Books.

Apte, M.L. (1985). *Humor and laughter: An anthropological approach*. Ithaca, NY: Cornell University Press.

Apter, M.J., & Smith, K.C.P. (1977). Humour and the theory of psychological reversals. In A.J. Chapman & H. Foot (Eds.), *It's a funny thing, humour*. Oxford: Pergamon.

Bandura, A. (1997). *Self-efficacy: The exercise of control*. New York: W.H. Freeman.

Beermann, U., & Ruch, W. (2009). How virtuous is humor? What we can learn from current instruments. *The Journal of Positive Psychology, 4*, 528-539.

Bell, N.J., McGhee, P.E., & Duffey, N.S. (1986). Interpersonal competence, social assertiveness and the development of humour. *British Journal of Developmental Psychology, 4*, 51-55.

Berger, A. (2010). What's so funny about that? *Society, 47*, 6-10.

Berlyne, D.E. (1972). Humor and its kin. In J.H. Goldstein & P.E. McGhee (Eds.), *The psychology of humor* (pp. 43-60). New York: Academic.

Bonanno, G.A., & Jost, J.T. (2006). Conservative shift among high-exposure survivors of the September 11th terrorist attacks. *Basic and Applied Social Psychology, 28*, 311 – 323.

Bond-Fraser, L., & Fraser, I. (February, 2010). *Generation Y and the use of humour, anecdote and real-world examples in the classroom.* Paper presented at the Annual Meeting of the American Association of Behavioral and Social Sciences, Las Vegas, Nevada.

Boyle, G.J., & Joss-Reid, J.M. (2004). Relationship of humour to health: A psychometric investigation. *British Journal of Health Psychology, 9*, 51-66.

Brock, A. (2004). Analyzing scripts in humorous communication. *HUMOR: International Journal of Humor Research, 17*, pp. 353–360.

Burridge, R.T. (1978). The nature and potential of therapeutic humor (Doctoral dissertation, California Institue of Asian Studies, 1978). *Dissertation Abstracts International, 39*, 2974.

Butovskaya, M., & Kozintsev, A. (1996). A neglected form of quasi-aggression in apes: possible relevance for the origins of humor. *Current Anthropology 37*, 716-717.

Caldwell, T.L., Cervone, D., & Rubin, L.H. (2008). Explaining intra-individual variability in social behavior through idiographic assessment: The case of humor. *Journal of Research in Personality, 42*, 1229-1242.

Cann, A., & Etzel, K.C. (2008). Remembering and anticipating stressors: Positive personality mediates the relationship with sense of humor. *Humor: International Journal of Humor Research, 21*, 157 – 178.

Cann, A., Holt, K., & Calhoun, L.G. (1999). The roles of humor and sense of humor in response to stressors. *Humor: International Journal of Humor Research, 12*, 177 – 193.

Carver, C.S. (1997). You want to measure coping but your protocol's too long: Consider the Brief COPE. *International Journal of Behavioral Medicine, 4,* 92-100.

Carver, C.S., Scheier, M.F., & Weintraub, J.K. (1989). Assessing coping strategies: A theoretical based approach. *Journal of Personality and Social Psychology, 56*, 267-283.

Cassell, J.L. (1974). The function of humor in the counseling process. *Rehabilitation Counseling Bulletin,* 240-245.

Cohen, J., Cohen, P., West, S.G., & Aiken, L.S. (2003). *Applied multiple regression/ correlational analysis for the behavioral sciences* (third edition). Mahwah, NJ: Lawrence Erlbaum Associates, Publishers.

Cohen, S., & Williamson, G. (1988). Perceived stress in a probability sample in the United States. In S. Spacapan & S. Oskamp (Eds.), *The social psychology of health* (pp. 31 – 67). Newbury Park, CA: Sage.

Comisky, P., Crane, J., & Zillmann, D. (1980). Relationship between college teachers' use of humor in the classroom and students' evaluations of their teachers. *Journal of Educational Psychology, 72*, 511-519.

Cook, T.D., & Campbell, D.T. (1970). *Quasi-experimentation: Design & Analysis issues for field settings.* Boston, MA: Houghton Mifflin Company.

Costa, P.T., & McCrae, R.R. (1992). *NEO-PI-R.* Odessa, FL: Psychological Assessment Resources.

Cousins, N. (1976). Anatomy of an illness: As perceived by the patient. *The New England Journal of Medicine, 295*, 1458-1463.

Cousins, N. (1979). *Anatomy of an illness as perceived by the patient: Reflections on healing and regeneration.* New York: Bantom Books.

Dean, R. A. (1997). Humor and laughter in palliative care. *Journal of Palliative Care, 13*, 34-39.

Deckers, L. (1998). Influence of mood on humor. In W. Ruch (ed.), *The sense of humor: Explorations of a personality characteristic.* Berlin, Germany: Mouton de Gruyter.

Delongis, A., Folkman, S., & Lazarus, R.S. (1988). The impact of daily stress on health and mood: Psychological and social resources as mediators. *Journal of Personality and Social Psychology, 54*(3), 486 – 495.

Diener, E., Wirtz, D., Tov, W., Kim-Prieto, C., Choi. D., Oishi, S., & Biswas-Diener, R. (2009). New measures of well-being: Flourishing and positive and negative feelings. *Social Indicators Research, 39,* 247-266.

Dixon, N.F. (1980). Humor: A cognitive alternative to stress? In I.G. Sarason & C.D. Spielberger (Eds.), *Stress and anxiety* (Vol. 7, pp. 281-289). Washington, DC: Hemisphere.

Dormann, C., & Biddle, R. (2006). Humor in game-based learning. *Learning, Media & Technology, 31,* 411-424.

Dunkelblau, E. (1987). "That'll be five cents, please!": Perceptions of psychotherapy in jokes and humor. In W.H. Fry and W.A. Fry, Jr. (Eds.), *Handbook of humor and psychotherapy: Advances in the clinical use of humor.* Sarasota, Florida: Professional Resource Exchange, Inc.

Durand, V.M. (1990). *Severe behavior problems: A functional communication training approach.* New York: Guilford Press.

Ellis, A. (1977). Fun as psychotherapy. *Rational Living, 12,* 2-6.

Epstein, R., & Joker, V.R. (2007). A threshold theory of the humor response. *The Behavior Analyst, 30,* 49-58.

Eysenck, H.J. (1942). The appreciation of humor: An experimental and theoretical study. *British Journal of Psychology, 32,* 295-309.

Eysenck, H.J. (1972). Forward. In J.H. Goldstein & P.E. McGhee (Eds.), *The psychology of humor.* New York: Academic Press.

Eysenck, H.J. (1997). Personality and experimental psychology: The unification of psychology and the possibility of a paradigm. *Journal of Personality and Social Psychology, 73,* 1224- 1237.

Feingold, A., & Maella, R. (1993). Preliminary validation of a multidimensional model of wittiness. *Journal of Personality, 61,* 439-456.

Ferguson, M.A., & Ford, T.E. (2008). Disparagement humor: A theoretical and empirical review of psychoanalytic, superiority, and social identity theories. *Humor: International Journal of Humor Research, 21,* 283-312.

Frazier, P.A., Tix, A.P., & Barron, K.E. (2004). Testing moderator and mediator effects in counseling psychology research. *Journal of Counseling Psychology, 51,* 115 – 134.

Freud, S. (1928). Humour. *International Journal of Psychoanalysis, 9*, 1-6.

Freud, S. (1936). *The problem of anxiety*. New York: The Psychoanalytic Quarterly Press and W.W. Norton and Company.

Freud, S. (1960[1905]). Jokes and their relation to the unconscious. New York: Norton.

Friedman, H.S. (2008). The multiple linkages of personality and disease. *Brain, Behavior, and Immunity, 22*, 668-675.

Friedman, H.S., Schwartz, J.E., Martin, L.R., Tomlinson-Keasey, C., Wingard, D.L., & Criqui, M.H. (1995). Chilhood conscientiusness and longevity: Health behaviors and cause of death. *Journal of Personality and Social Psychlogy, 68,* 696-703.

Friedman, H.S., Tucker, J.S., Tomlinson-Keasey, C., Schwartz, J.E., Wingard, D.L., & Criqui, M.H. (1993). Does childhood personality predict longevity? *Journal of Personality and Social Psychology, 65*, 176-185.

Fry, P.S. (1995). Perfectionism, humor, and optimism as moderators of health outcomes and determinants of coping styles of women executives. *Genetic, Social, and General Psychology Monographs, 121*, 211 – 245.

Fry, W.F. (1994). The biology of humor. *Humor: International Journal of Humor Research, 7*, 111-126.

Giuliani, N.R., McRae, K., & Gross, J.J. (2008). The up- and down-regulation of amusement: Experiential, behavioral, and autonomic consequences. *Emotion, 8*, 714 – 719.

Goldstein, J.H. (1987). Therapeutic effects of laughter. In W.H. Fry and W.A. Salameh (Eds.), *Handbook of humor and psychotherapy: Advances in the clinical use of humor*. Sarasota, Florida: Professional Resource Exchange, Inc.

Gollob, H.F., & Levine, J. (1967). Distraction as a factor in the enjoyment of aggressive humor. *Journal of Personality and Social Psychology, 5*, 368-372.

Grieg, J.Y.T. (1969). *The psychology of laughter and comedy*. New York: Cooper Square Publishers, Inc.

Grossman, S.A. (1977). The use of jokes in psychotherapy. In A.J. Chapman and H.C. Foot (Eds.), *Its' a funny thing, humour*. New York: Pergamon Press.

Gruner, C.R. (1997). *The game of humor: A comprehensive theory of why we laugh*. New Brunswick, NJ: Transaction Publishers.

Haig, R.A. (1988). *The anatomy of humor: Biopsychosocial and therapeutic perspectives*. Springfield, IL: Thomas.

Hehl, F.J., & Ruch, W. (1985). The location of sense of humor within comprehensive personality spaces: An exploratory study. *Personality and Individual Differences, 6*, 703 – 715.

Herzog, T.R., & Strevey, S.J. (2008). Contact with nature, sense of humor, and psychological well-being. *Environment and Behavior, 40*, 747-776.

Hulse, J. R. (1994). Humor: a nursing intervention for the elderly. *Geriatric Nursing, 15*, 88-90.

Kanner, A.D., Coyne, J.C., Schaefer, C., & Lazarus, R.S. (1981). Comparison of two modes of stress measurement: Daily hassles and uplifts versus major life events. *Journal of Behavioral Medicine, 41* – 39.

Kant, I. (1952 [1790]). *The critique of judgement*. Oxford: Clarendon Press.

Kerkkänen, P., Kuiper, N.A., & Martin, R.A. (2004). Sense of humor, physical health, and well- being at work: A three-year longitudinal study of Finnish police officers. *Humor: International Journal of Humor Research, 17*, 21 – 35.

Klein, A. (1989). *The healing power of humor*. Los Angeles: Jeremy P. Tarcher, Inc.

Kline, P. (1977). The psychoanalytic theory of humour and laughter. In A.J. Chapman & H.C. Foot (Eds.), *It's a funny thing, humour*. Oxford: Pergamon Press.

Kobasa, S.C.O. (1979). Personality and resistance to illness. American Journal of Community Psychology, *7*, 413-422.

Koestler, A. (1964). *The act of creation*. London: Hutchinson.

Kohn, P.M., Lafreniere, K., & Gurevich, M. (1990). The Inventory of College Students' Recent Life Experiences: A decontaminated hassles scale for a special population. *Journal of Behavioral Medicine, 13*, 616 – 630.

Korotkov, D. (1991). An exploratory factor analysis of the sense of humour personality construct: A pilot project. *Personality and Individual Differences, 12*, 395-397.

Korotkov, D. (2000). *Measuring hassles and physical symptomatology.* Unpublished manuscript. Korotkov, D. (2010). *Demographic measurement.* Unpublished manuscript.

Korotkov, D., & Hannah, T.E. (1994). Extraversion and emotionality as proposed superordinate stress moderators: A prospective analysis. *Personality and Individual Differences, 16*, 787- 792.

Korotkov, D. (2010a). *Extraverted and energized: A Review and tests of stress moderation and mediation.* New York: Nova Science Publishers.

Korotkov, D. (2010b). Extraversion, daily life stress, perceived energy, and health: A review and tests of stress moderation and mediation. In A.M. Columbus (ed.), *Advances in psychology research* (Vol. 70). New York: Nova Science Publishers.

Kozma, A., Stones, M.J., & McNeil, K. (1991). *Psychological well-being in later life.* Toronto: Butterworth.

Kuiper, N.A., & Borowicz-Sibenik, M. (2005). A good sense of humor doesn't always help: Agency and communion as moderators of psychological well-being. *Personality and Individual Differences, 38*, 365-377.

Kuiper, N.A., Grimshaw, M., Leite, C., & Kirsh, G. (2004). Humor is not always the best medicine: Specific components of sense of humor and psychological well-being. *Humor: International Journal of Humor Research, 17*, 135-168.

Kuiper, N.A., & Martin, R.A. (1998). Is sense of humor a positive personality characteristic? In W. Ruch (ed.), *The sense of humor: Explorations of a personality construct* (pp. 159-178). Berlin: Mouton de Gruyter.

Kuiper, N.A., Martin, R.A., & Dance, K.A. (1992). Sense of humour and enhanced quality of life. *Personality and Individual Differences, 13,* 1273-1283.

Kuiper, N.A., Martin, R.A., & Olinger, L.J. (1993). Coping humour, stress, and cognitive appraisals. *Canadian Journal of Behavioural Science, 25,* 81-96.

Kuiper, N.A., & Nicholl, S. (2004). Thoughts of feeling better? Sense of humor and physical health. *Humor: International Journal of HumorResearch, 17,* 37 – 66.

Kulpers, G. (2006). *Good Humor, Bad Taste: A Sociology of the Joke.* Berlin–New York: Mouton de Gruyter.

Lazarus, R.S., & Folkman, S. (1984). *Stress, appraisal, and coping.* New York: Springer Publishing Company.

Lee, Y.H., & Lim, E.A.C. (2008). What's funny and what's not: The moderating role of cultural orientation in ad humor. *Journal of Advertising, 37,* 71-84.

Lefcourt, H.M., & Martin, R.A. (1986). *Humor and life stress: Antidote to adversity.* New York: Springer-Verlag.

Lefcourt, H.M., & Thomas, S. (1998). Humor and stress revisited. In W. Ruch (ed.), *The sense of humor: Explorations of a personality construct.* Berlin: Mouton de Gruyter.

Lehman, K.M., Burke, K.L., Martin, R., Sultan, J., & Czech, D.R. (2001). A reformulation of the moderating effects of productive humor. *Humor: International Journal of Humor Research, 14,* 131-161.

Levine, J. (1969). *Motivation in humor.* New York: Atherton Press.

Levine, J., & Rakusin, J. (1959). The sense of humor of college students and psychiatric patients. *The Journal of General Psychology, 60,* 183 – 190.

Lewis, P. (2006). *Cracking up: American humor in a time of conflict.* Chicago, IL: Unversity fo Chicago Press.

Luiselli, J.K., & Cameron, M.J. (1998). *Antecedent control: Innovative approaches to behavioral support.* Baltimore, Maryland: Paul H. Brookes Publishing Co.

Lyubomirsky, S., & Lepper, H.S. (1999). A measure of subjective happiness: Preliminary reliability and construct validation. *Social Indicators Research, 46,* 137-155.

MacKinnon, D.P. (2008). *Introduction to statistical mediation analysis.* New York: Lawrence Erlbaum Associates.

MacMillan, A.M. (1957). The Health Opinion Survey: Technique for estimating prevalence of psychoneurotic and related types of disorder in communities. *Psychological Reports, 3,* 325- 339.

Marshall, G.N., Wortman, C.B., Vickers, Jr., Kusulas, J.W., & Hervig, L.K. (1994). The Five- Factor Model of Personality as a framework for personality-health research. *Journal of Personality and Social Psychology, 67,* 278-286.

Martin, R.A. (1996). The Situational Humor Response Questionnaire (SHRQ) and Coping Humor Scale (CHS): A decade of research findings. *Humor: International Journal of Humor Research, 9,* 251 – 272.

Martin, L.R., Friedman, H.S., Tucker, J.S., Tomlinson-Keasey, C., Criqui, H., & Schwartz, J.E. (2003). A life course perspective on childhood cheerfulness and its relation to mortality risk. *Personality and Social Psychology Bulletin, 28,* 1155-1165.

Martin, R.A. (2001). Humor, laughter, and physical health: Methodological issues and research findings. *Psychological Bulletin, 127,* 504 – 519.

Martin, R.A. (2002). Is laughter the best medicine? Humor, laughter, and physical health. *Current Directions in Psychological Science, 11,* 216-220.

Martin, R.A. (2003). Sense of humor. In S.J. Lopez & C.R. Snyder (Eds.), *Positive psychological assessment: A handbook of models and measures* (pp. 313-326). Washington, DC: American Psychological Association.

Martin, R.A. (2007). *The psychology of humor: An integrative approach.* London, UK: Elsevier Academic Press.

Martin, R.A., & Dobbin, J.P. (1988). Sense of humor, hassles, and immunoglobulin A: Evidence for a stress-moderating effect of humor. *International Journal of Psychiatry in Medicine, 18,* 93 – 105.

Martin, R.A., & Lefcourt, H.M. (1984). Situational Humor Response Questionnaire: Quantitative measure of sense of humor. *Journal of Personality and Social Psychology, 47*, 145 – 155.

Martin, R.A., & Lefcourt, H.M. (1983). The sense of humor as a moderator of the relationship between stressors and moods. *Journal of Personality and Social Psychology, 45*, 1313 – 1324.

Martin, G., & Pear, J. (2011). *Behavior modification: What it is and how to do it.* Upper Saddle River, New Jersey: Pearson – Prentice Hall.

Martin, R.A., Puhlik-Doris, P., Larsen, G., Gray, J., & Weir, K. (2003). Individual differences in uses of humor and their relation to psychological well-being: Development of the Humor Styles Questionnaire. *Journal of Research in Personality, 37*, 48 – 75.

McCrae, R.R., & Costa Jr., P.T. (1985). Updating Norman's 'adequate taxonomy': Intelligence and personality dimensions in natural language and in questionnaires. *Journal of Personality and Social Psychology, 49*, 710 – 721.

McGhee, P.E. (1979). *Humor: Its origin and development.* San Francisco: Freeman.

McNeil, J.K. (1987). *Mood: Measurement, diurnal variation and age effects.* Unpublished doctoral dissertation, Memorial University of Newfoundland, St. John's, Newfoundland.

Meyer, J.C. (1997), Humor in member narratives: Uniting and dividing the work. *Western Journal of Communication, 61*, 188-208.

Mihalcea, R., & Strapparava, C. (2006). Learning to laugh (automatically): Computational models for humor recognition. *Computational Intelligence, 22*, 126-142.

Mik-Meyer, N. (2007). Interpersonal relations or jokes of social structure? Laughter in social work. *Qualitative Social Work: Research and Practice, 6*, 9-26.

Miltenberger, R.G. (2008). *Behavior modification: Principles and procedures.* Belmont, CA: Thomson Wadsworth.

Mindess, H., Miller, C., Turek, J., Bender, A., & Corbin, S. (1985). *The Antioch Humor Test: Making sense of humor.* New York: Avon.

Moody, R. (1978). *Laugh after laugh: The healing power of humor*. Jacksonville, FL: Headwaters Press.

Moran, C.C., & Hughes, L.P. (2006). Coping with stress: Social work students and humour. *Social Work Education, 25,* 501 – 517.

Morris, J.S. (2009). The Daily Show with Jon Stewart and audience attitude change during the 2004 party conventions. *Political Behavior, 31,* 79-102.

Nahemow, L., McCluskey-Fawcett, K.A., & McGhee, P.A. (1986). *Humor and aging*. Orlando, Florida: Academic Press.

Nerhardt, G. (1976). Incongruity and funniness: Towards a new descriptive model. In A.J. Chapman & H.C. Foot (Eds.), *Humour and laughter: Theory, research, and applications*. (pp. 55-62) London: Wiley.

Nevo, O., Aharonson, H., & Klingman, A. (1998). The development and evaluation of a systematic program for improving sense of humor. In W. Ruch (ed.), *The sense of humor: Explorations of a personality characteristic*. New York: Mouton de Gruyter.

O'Connell, W.E. (1976). Freudian humour: The eupsychia of everyday life. In A.J. Chapman & H.C. Foot (Eds.), *Humour and laughter: Theory, research, and applications*. London: Wiley.

O'Neill, R.E., Horner, R.H., Albin, R.W., Sprague, J.R., Storey, K., & Newton, J.S. (1997). *Functional assessment and program development for problem behavior: A practical handbook*. Pacific Grove, CA: Brooks/Cole Publishing Company.

Oring, E. (1992). *Jokes and their relations*. Lexington: The University Press of Kentucky.

Peter, L.J., & Dana, B. (1982). *The laughter prescription*. New York: Ballantine Books.

Peterson, C., & Seligman, M.E.P. (2004). *Character strengths and virtues: A handbook and classification*. Washington, DC: American Psychological Association.

Rakel, D.P., & Hedgecock, J. (2008). Healing the healer: A tool to encourage student reflection towards health. *Medical Teacher, 30,* 633-635.

Richman, J. (1996). Points of correspondence between humor and psychotherapy. *Psychotherapy: Theory, Research, Practice, Training, 33,* 560-566.

Roberts, B.W., Kuncel, N.R., Shiner, R., Caspi, A., & Goldberg, L.R. (2007). The power of personality: The comparative validity of personality traits, socioeconomic status, and cognitive ability for predicting important life outcomes. *Perspectives on Psychological Science, 2,* 313-345.

Rogerson-Revell, P. (2007). Humour in business: A double-edged sword. A study of humour and style shifting in intercultural business meetings. *Journal of Pragmatics, 39,* 4-28.

Ruch, W. (1992). Assessment of appreciation of humor: Studies with the 3 WD Humor Test, in Charles D. Spielberger & James Butcher (eds.), *Advances in personality assessment* (Vol. 9). Hillsdale, NJ: Erlbaum.

Ruch, W. (1998a). *The sense of humor: Explorations of a personality characteristic.* Berlin, Germany: Mouton de Gruyter.

Ruch, W. (1998b). Sense of humor: A new look at an old concept. In W. Ruch (ed.), *The sense of humor: Explorations of a personality characteristic.* Berlin, Germany: Mouton de Gruyter.

Ruch, W., & Deckers, L. (1993). Do extraverts "like to laugh"? An analysis of the Situational Humor Response Questionnaire (SHRQ). *European Journal of Personality, 7,* 211-220.

Ruch, W., Kohler, G., & van Thriel, L. (1997).To be in good or bad humor: Construction of the State-Trait-Cheerfulness-Inventory-STCI. *Personality and Individual Differences, 22,* 477-491.

Salvatore, A. (1994). *Linguistic theories of humor.* Berlin–New York: Mouton de Gruyter.

Saroglou, V., & Scariot, C. (2002). Humor Styles Questionnaire: Personality and educational correlates in Belgian high school and college students. *European Journal of Personality, 16,* 43 – 54.

Scheier, M.F., & Carver, C.S. (1985). Optimism, coping, and health: Assessment and implications of generalized outcome expectancies. *Health Psychology, 4,* 219 – 247.

Semrud-Clikeman, M., & Glass, K. (2008). Comprehension of humor in children with nonverbal learning disabilities, reading disabilities, and without learning disabilities. *Annals of Dyslexia, 58*, 163-180.

Simon, J.M. (1988). Humour and the older adult: Implications for nursing. *Journal of Advanced Nursing, 13*, 441 – 446.

Simon, R.K. (1977). Freud's concepts of comedy and suffering. *Psychoanalytic Review, 64*, 391-407.

Sulloway, F.J. (1979). *Freud, biologist of the mind: Beyond the psychoanalytic legend.* New York: Basic Books.

Suls, J.M. (1972). A two-stage model for the appreciation of jokes and cartoons. In J.H. Goldstein and P.E. McGree (eds.), *The psychology of humor.* 81-100. New York: Academic Press.

Suls, J.M. (1983). Cognitive processes in humor appreciation. In P.E. McGhee & J.H. Goldstein (Eds.), *Handbook of humor research* (Vol. 1, pp. 39-58). New York: Springer Verlag.

Sundel, M., & Stone Sundel, S. (1975). *Behavior modification in the human services.* New York: John Wiley & Sons.

Sundel, S., & Sundel, M. (1993). *Behavior modification in the human services.* Newbury Park: Sage Publications.

Svebak, S. (1974). Revised questionnaire on the sense of humor. *Scandinavian Journal of Psychology, 15*, 328 – 331.

Svebak, S. (1996). The development of the Sense of Humor Questionnaire: From SHQ to SHQ- 6. *Humor: International Journal of Humor Research, 9*, 341 – 361.

Svebak, S. (2010). The Sense of Humor Questionnaire: Conceptualization and review of 40 years of findings in empirical research. *Europe's Journal of Psychology, 3*, 288-310.

Svebak, S., Götestam, K.G., & Jensen, E.N. (2004). The significance of humor, life regard, and stressors for bodily complaints among high school students. *Humor: International Journal of Humor Research, 17*, 67 – 83.

Svebak, S., Jensen, E.N., & Götestam, K.G. (2008). Some health effects of implementing school nursing in a Norwegian high school: A controlled study. *The Journal of School Nursing, 24*, 49 – 54.

Svebak, S., Kristoffersen, B., & Aasarød, K. (2006). Sense of humor and survival among a county cohort of patients with end-stage renal failure: A two-year prospective study. *International Journal of Psychiatry in Medicine, 36,* 269-281.

Svebak, S., Martin, R.A., & Holmen, J. (2004). The prevalence of sense of humor in a large, unselected county population in Norway: Relations with age, sex, and some health indicators. *Humor: International Journal of HumorResearch, 17,* 121 – 134.

Thorson, J.A., & Powell, F.C. (1993). Development and validation of a multidimensional sense of humor scale. *Journal of Clinical Psychology, 49,* 13 – 23.

Tümkaya, S. (2007). Burnout and humor relationship among university lecturers. *Humor: International Journal of Humor Research, 20,* 73 – 92.

Turner, R.G. (1980). Self-monitoring and humor production. *Journal of Personality, 48,* 163-172.

Vaillant, G.E. (2000). Adaptive mental mechanisms: Their role in positive psychology. *American Psychologist, 55,* 89-98.

Ventis, W.L., Higbee, G., & Murdock, S.A. (2001). Using humor in systematic desensitization to reduce fear. *Journal of General Psychology, 128,* 241-253.

Vollrath, M. (2001). Personality and stress. *Scandinavian Journal of Psychology, 42,* 335-347.

Watson, K.K., Matthews, B.J., & Allman, J.M. (2007). Brain activation during sight gags and language-dependent humor. *Cerebral Cortex, 17,* 314-324.

Wiebe, D.J., & Fortenberry, K.T. (2006). Mechanisms relating personality and health. In M.E. Vollrath (ed.), *Handbook of personality and health* (pp. 137-156). West Sussex: John Wiley & Sons Ltd.

Wyer, R.S., & Collins, J.E. (1992). A theory of humor elicitation. *Psychological Review, 99,* 663-688.

Zigler, E., Levine, J., & Gould, L. (1966). Cognitive processes in the development of children's appreciation of humor. *Child Development, 37,* 507-518.

Zijderveld, A.C. (1995). Humor, laughter, and sociological theory. *Sociological Forum, 10*, 341-345.

Ziv, A (1979). The teacher's sense of humour and the atmosphere in the classroom. *School Psychology International, 1*, 21-23.

Ziv, A. (1984). *Personality and sense of humor*. New York: Springer.

Zweyer, K., Velker, B., & Ruch, W. (2004). Do cheerfulness, exhilaration, and humor production moderate pain tolerance? A FACS study. *Humor: International Journal of Humor Research, 17*, 85-119.

BIOGRAPHIES

Dr. Dave Korotkov is an Associate Professor of Psychology at St. Thomas University in Fredericton, New Brunswick, Canada. He obtained his BA from Brock University and PhD from Memorial University of Newfoundland. His research interests include the role of personality in relation to stress, health behavior, and health, time perspective, the doctor-patient relationship, and behavioral assessment. He has taught courses in health psychology, community psychology, environmental psychology, social psychology, behavior modification, research methods, and statistics.

Dr. Mihailo Perunovic obtained his BA from York University and his PhD from the University of Waterloo. He is currently an Assistant Professor in the Department of Psychology at St. Thomas University. His main areas of research in psychology are in social/personality psychology, as well as romantic relationships. He teaches courses in introductory psychology, biological psychology, personality, and relationships.

Dr. Marvin Claybourn (PhD, L.Psych.) is an Assistant Professor in the Department of Psychology at St. Thomas University as well as a practicing clinician. Dr. Claybourn received his PhD from the University of New Brunswick. His research interests are focused on the individual and environmental factors that contribute to the understanding of the interconnectedness of physical and mental health. Dr. Claybourn has taught such courses as statistics and research methods, I/O psychology, sexuality, social psychology, and personality.

Dr. Ian Fraser graduated from the University of Aberdeen, Scotland in 1986 with a PhD in perceptual psychology. He is currently a Full Professor of Psychology at St. Thomas University in Fredericton, New Brunswick. His research interests include the impacts of teaching anxiety on the university professor, perception, and eyewitness testimony. He teaches courses in introductory psychology, as well as perception, and psychology of the law.

AUTHORS' NOTE

The authors would like to thank Kimberly Korotkov for reviewing this manuscript, Lauren Hamilton for assisting in the collection of data for Study 3, and Erika Montero for the data entry portion of Study 3.

INDEX